INTRODUCTION

When German forces initiated Operation Barbarossa on 22 June 1941 and the assault on the Soviet Union began, the *Luftwaffe* enjoyed almost total supremacy in Soviet skies. The fighter element of the Soviet Air Forces, or *Voenno-vozdushniye Sily* (V-VS), was immersed in a major re-equipment programme resulting from belated appreciation by the Soviet leadership of the fact that its aircraft had fallen woefully behind world standard. Immense effort had been directed towards rectifying this situation in the two years immediately preceding Soviet involvement in World War II. New fighter designs had been hastily committed to large-scale production by a dramatically expanding aircraft industry which perforce employed a very high proportion of semi-skilled and unskilled labour; fighters suffering defects that were an inevitable consequence of the hurried tempo of their development; defects compounded by low manufacturing standards that were equally inevitable in so rapidly expanding an industry. The shortcomings of this new generation of fighters posed serious problems for the V-VS and these, exacerbated by the inadequacies of Soviet fighter pilot training, contributed substantially to the decimation of the V-VS fighter regiments in the opening phases of what the Soviet Union chose to call the "Great Patriotic War".

This new generation of fighters comprised the progeny of newly created and thus relatively inexperienced design bureaux, and wartime development of the single-seat fighter in the Soviet Union was to be characterised by the continuous refinement of two fundamental designs bearing the appellations of Lavochkin and Yakovlev. While other major combatants were to phase into service entirely new fighter types as the conflict progressed, the Soviet Union alone was unable to afford such luxury; all effort had to be directed towards maximising fighter output and the disruption of assembly lines and ensuing loss of production associated with the introduction of totally new aircraft were not to be tolerated. Thus, frontline demands for improvements in fighter capability to compensate for changing operational conditions and progressively more advanced enemy warplanes as they were committed to the air war over the Soviet Union had to be accommodated by a process of continuous refinement of existing aircraft.

These aircraft were essentially simple to manufacture and easy to repair in the field; they were thoroughly orthodox in concept and of wooden or wood-and-steel-tube construction with fabric and plywood skinning. By western standards they were austerely equipped and they were built in very large numbers with upwards of 60,000 being delivered from 1941 until the end of hostilities. Despite the substantial production quantities of these aircraft, however, there was little standardisation, minor differences appearing on individual aircraft of even small production batches. This resulted from the serious shortage of skilled labour throughout the aircraft industry and the considerable confusion that prevailed — the individual sub-contracting plants supplying components, assemblies etc., frequently working to different tolerances and ignoring fine measurements — and the fact that a considerable amount of handwork was applied on the final assembly line (e.g., skin panels, cover plates, joints, etc., being trimmed or shaped to fit an individual aircraft, interchangeability thus becoming limited). While a main plant, on occasions, switched to a new sub-type of the fighter that it was manufacturing, the sub-contractors as likely as not continued the manufacture of parts for the preceding sub-type owing to the previously-mentioned confusion, with the result that these had to be adapted on the main assembly line. Thus, it was possible for the individual aircraft of one production batch to embody different wings, cockpit frames, armament, internal equipment, etc.

By the standards of the day, the materials and constructional methods employed in the manufacture of Soviet wartime fighters were primitive, but the use of more modern light-alloy stressed-skin structures was not within the capabilities of the Soviet aircraft industry at the time, apart from the fact that such were ruled out by the Soviet Union's chronic shortage of light alloys. However, if Soviet fighters were to be adjudged rudimentary by enemies and allies alike, they were to prove ideally suited to the conditions under which they were forced to operate; conditions that would have grounded their more sophisticated western contemporaries. Their simple, thoroughly orthodox concept was deceptive in that it suggested that Soviet fighter designers lacked creativity, whereas, in fact, they were no less innovative than their western counterparts, but their inventiveness was subjugated by the exigencies of the times. Indeed, although Soviet designers were largely pre-occupied with the development of combat aircraft that were simple to manufacture, maintain and fly, some highly innovatory ideas *did* reach the flight test stage. For example, under the aegis of Professor Viktor Bolkhovitinov the world's first rocket-propelled interceptor fighter was flown and the series of variable-geometry or "folding" fighters created by the design bureau led by Vasili Nikitin must surely be numbered among the most ingenious fighters of their era. Again, such mixed-power fighters as the I-250(N) developed by the Mikoyan-Gurevich bureau to utilise Khalshchevnikov's so-called "accelerator" were far removed from what was considered the conventional.

This first part of a two-part *Fact File* devoted to all types of indigenous fighter operated by or developed to experimental status for the Soviet Air Forces is primarily concerned with the products of the design bureaux led by Semyon A.Lavochkin and the partnership of Artem I.Mikoyan and Mikhail I. Gurevich, whose fighters, when first opposed by the *Luftwaffe* enjoyed indifferent success. Whereas the Mikoyan-Gurevich team largely concentrated its wartime efforts on creating specialised high-altitude fighters which were to receive low development priority owing to more pressing needs, Lavochkin was to overcome early setbacks and achieve outstanding success by the continuous refinement of one basic design; a process epitomized by the La-7 which played a major role in the closing stages of the Second World (or "Great Patriotic") War.

One of the more radical fighters evolved in the Soviet Union during World War II was the rocket-propelled BI target-defence interceptor, the first prototype airframe of which, completed in glider form, being illustrated below and at the head of the opposite page. Completed within 35 days of the first wood being cut, the first BI airframe was fitted with water ballast tanks approximating to the weight of the proposed power plant, fuel and armament. Gliding trails with this aircraft began in September 1941, and is seen here at the design bureau's experimental shops near Moscow prior to their evacuation in the face of the advancing Wehrmacht. Boris N. Kudrin, who was assigned to the programme as senior pilot, is seen with the aircraft in the photograph below

BEREZNYAK-ISAEV (BOLKHOVITINOV) BI

Between the two World Wars, consideration was given desultorily in several countries to the potential of the liquid-fuel rocket motor as a means of propelling a warhead, but methodical and persistent investigation of its possibilities as a means of aircraft propulsion was confined to the Soviet Union and Germany. Elsewhere, the combination of manned airframe and rocket motor was viewed with much scepticism; a dangerous stunt rather than a practical means of powering an aircraft. Inordinately high fuel consumption and the hazards inherent in handling and storing rocket fuels notwithstanding, the unique properties of the liquid-fuel rocket motor were considered sufficiently attractive by Soviet and German design teams to warrant concerted effort towards applying such propulsive units to manned airframes and, specifically, short-range interceptor fighters.

In so far as the Soviet Union was concerned, major effort on rocket propulsion had dated from 1934 with the creation by Marshal Tukhachevsky, C-in-C of the Soviet Armed Forces, of the RNII — *Reaktivnyi Nauchno-issledovatelsky institut*, or Reaction Engine Scientific Research Institute. Tukhachevsky had been convinced that the rocket had a major role to play in warfare and the newly-created institute was intended to co-ordinate work on rocket propulsion previously conducted independently by the Rocket Propulsion Study Group (GIRD) in Moscow and the Gas Dynamics Laboratory (GDL) in Leningrad, pursuing a broad-based programme which was to include investigation of the use of such fuels as powdered aluminium, the auto-stabilization of rockets, the development of smokeless powder rockets with warheads as air-to-air and air-to-surface weapons, and for surface-to-surface saturation bombardment, and the development of liquid-propellant rocket motors of both fixed and variable thrust.

While emphasis was placed primarily on the potential of the rocket for missile propulsion, during 1936, the deputy scientific director of the RNII, S.P.Korolev, together with Ye.S.Shchetinkov, initiated a highly ambitious design programme for a rocket-propelled research aircraft, the RP-218 and, in a paper entitled "Scientific Research Work in Rocket Techniques" published in February 1938, promoted the rocket motor as a prime mover for fighter aircraft. While the RP-218 design outstripped Soviet technology of the day and, in consequence, was never built, a somewhat less ambitious programme was launched entailing the adaptation of a two-seat SK-9 sailplane for rocket propulsion.

Valentin Glushko had, meanwhile, undertaken much basic research in the development of liquid-propellant rocket motors, using alcohol, petroleum or kerosene as fuel with nitric acid as an oxidant, and testing units with thrusts ranging from 176 to 1,320 pounds (80 to 600 kg), and one of these units, the 385 lb (175 kg) ORM-65 using kerosene and nitric acid, was selected for installation in the Korolev-designed sailplane, which, in rocket-driven form, was assigned the designation RP-318. The task of converting the SK-9 as the RP-318 was assigned to Aleksis Ya.Shcherbakov and Arvid V.Pallo, but work proceeded slowly in order to parallel the bench testing of the ORM-65 rocket which was demonstrating unstable characteristics. The poor reliability of this power plant was such that, eventually, it was discarded in favour of another rocket motor, the RDA-1-150, which, developed by two other members of the RNII team, Leonid S. Dushkin and Aleksei M.Isaev*, offered the advantage of controllable thrust. Weighing 220 lb (100 kg) and affording a

---
*Aleksei Isaev was, many years later, to be primarily responsible for the design of the power plant of the Vostok, Voskhod and Soyus space launching vehicles.

maximum thrust of 330 lb (150 kg), the RDA-1-150 was installed in the extreme tail of the RP-318, the fuel and oxidant tanks being mounted immediately aft of the pilot's cockpit. With 165 lb (75 kg) of fuel, sufficient for 100 seconds burning at full thrust, the RP-318 weighed 1,543 lb (700 kg).

Powered flights began on 28 February 1940, after the pilot, Vladimir P.Fedorov, had performed 16 preliminary trials with water ballast in place of the fuel and oxidant. These trials were so successful that plans were prepared to install a 661 lb (300 kg) thrust rocket motor in the RP-318 airframe, which, it was anticipated, would provide sufficient power to enable the aircraft to take-off from a jettisonable trolley. In the event, these plans were to be thwarted by the discovery that the airframe had suffered damage as a result of corrosion.

Two of the RP-318 powered trials had been witnessed by Aleksandr Ya.Bereznyak, an aerodynamicist working under Professor Viktor F. Bolkhovitinov at the Zhukovsky Academy, who was immediately fascinated by the potential that he believed rocket propulsion to display. By this time, Dushkin and Isaev, assisted by A.V.Pallo, V.A.Shtokolov and A.P.Sheptitsky, were engaged in the development of a substantially more powerful rocket motor based on experience gained with the RDA-1-150. Envisaged primarily as a propulsion unit for a heavy missile and as a possible auxiliary booster unit for combat aircraft, this, the D-1A-1100, was expected to provide a thrust of 2,425 lb (1 100 kg), and when told of this new power plant by Aleksei Isaev, Bereznyak immediately conceived the idea of designing a small target-defence interceptor fighter around the new rocket motor, totally unaware that a warplane of essentially similar concept was at that time being considered in Germany.

Bereznyak succeeded in arousing the interest of his mentor, Professor Bolkhovitinov, in his idea, and the latter, after discussions with Isaev, was sufficiently convinced of the viability of the proposal to place it before the *Narkomavprom* — the State Commissariat of the Aviation Industry — with his recommendation that the scheme be pursued. The innovatory nature of the concept captured the imagination of no less a person than Yosif Stalin, and not only did the project receive official blessing — an official requirement was drawn up around Bolkhovitinov's outline proposal to enable other design bureaux to consider this audacious scheme.

Detail design of the rocket-propelled fighter began on the drawing boards at the Zhukovsky Academy in the spring of 1941 under the overall supervision of Professor Bolkhovitinov, the project being known simply as the BI, these letters standing for Bereznyak and Isaev who were primarily responsible for both the concept and the design. On 22 June 1941 — the day on which the *Wehrmacht* assault on the Soviet Union was launched — authorisation was given by the *Minaviaprom* (Ministry of the Aviation Industry) for the construction of five prototypes to commence in a factory on the outskirts of Moscow. The BI was aerodynamically a clean little aeroplane, apart from rather ungainly tail surfaces, and featured an oval-section semi-monocoque wooden fuselage with plywood skinning and an outer covering of doped fabric, a similarly-covered two-spar wooden wing and fixed tail surfaces. The entire trailing edge of the wing was occupied by metal-framed fabric-covered ailerons and pneumatically-operated dural-skinned split flaps. The mainwheels retracted inwards into wells in the base of the fuselage, all three undercarriage members being pneumatically operated. The D-1A-1100 rocket motor, which measured only 12.6 in (32 cm) in diameter and 31.5 in (80 cm) in overall length, was mounted in the tail of the fuselage and to achieve a satisfactory CG range, the kerosene tank was installed in the fuselage nose, ahead of the cockpit, together with the compressed air cylinders for the pneumatic systems, the radio and the armament, and the nitric acid tanks were installed immediately aft of the cockpit. No armour

The second prototype airframe of the BI interceptor which was fitted with retractable skis. During pre-flight trials of this aircraft, the rocket combustion chamber exploded and a number of the test personnel were burned by the oxidant, test pilot Bakhchivandzhe being injured

protection was provided for the pilot, whose tiny cockpit was enclosed by an aft-sliding single-piece canopy, and provision was made for a pair of 20-mm ShVAK cannon with 45 rounds per gun.

A special BI task force had been formed to develop the rocket-propelled fighter in the minimum possible time, its principal members being A.Ye.Roslyanov as chief engineer with Arvid Pallo — who had shared responsibility for conversion of the SK-9 sailplane as the RP-318 — as his assistant, Col.Eng.M.I.Tarakanovsky from the NII V-VS — *Nauchno-issledovatelsky institut V-VS*, or Scientific Research Institute of the Air Forces — who was assigned responsibility for preparing the BI for its initial flight test programme, and A.S.Sorokin and A.A.Kolesnikov from the RNII. The oldest active test pilot in the Soviet Union, Boris N.Kudrin, was assigned to the programme as senior pilot, and thanks to its simplicity, the first airframe was completed within 35 days of the first wood being cut. Completed as a glider with water ballast tanks to simulate power plant, fuel and armament, this was towed into the air behind a Pe-2 light bomber on 10 September 1941 with Kudrin at the controls.

While gliding trials proceeded, the second and third airframes were being prepared for testing with the rocket motor, but the *Wehrmacht* was by now approaching Moscow — Marshal Fedor von Bock's Army Group Centre had reached Mozhaisk, 40 miles (64 km) from the Soviet capital by 20 October — and the hurried evacuation of the factory in which the BI prototypes were being built became urgently necessary, the project being transferred to a partly-completed iron foundry at Koltsova, in the vicinity of Sverdlovsk. Kudrin had meanwhile been taken ill and a former NII V-VS engineering test pilot, Grigori Ya.Bakhchivandzhe, who was flying with a fighter IAP of the Moscow PVO, was recalled to the NII V-VS and assigned to the BI programme. Bakhchivandzhe had, in July 1937, performed a successful series of launching trials with experimental 82-mm air-to-air rockets developed at the RNII by its first director and chief scientist, Ivan T.Kleimenov, and the Institute's chief engineer, Georgi A.Langemak (these missiles having subsequently entered production as the RS-82), and had maintained an interest in rocket propulsion. Unfortunately, on 20 February 1942, while performing pre-flight ground testing of the first BI airframe to be fitted with the D-1A-1100 rocket, Bakhchivandzhe inadvertently opened the throttle too rapidly and the combustion chamber exploded. Arvid Pallo and two other test personnel were badly burned by the oxidant and Bakhchivandzhe was thrown forward violently in the cockpit, hitting his head and suffering concussion. Nevertheless, he recovered sufficiently to perform powered trials as soon as the third airframe could be readied.

Taxying trials under power began during the first week of May at the airfield adjacent to the factory, and during the last of these, Bakhchivandzhe lifted the BI off the runway and flew about 55 yards (50 m) in a straight line a few feet above the runway. As the airfield

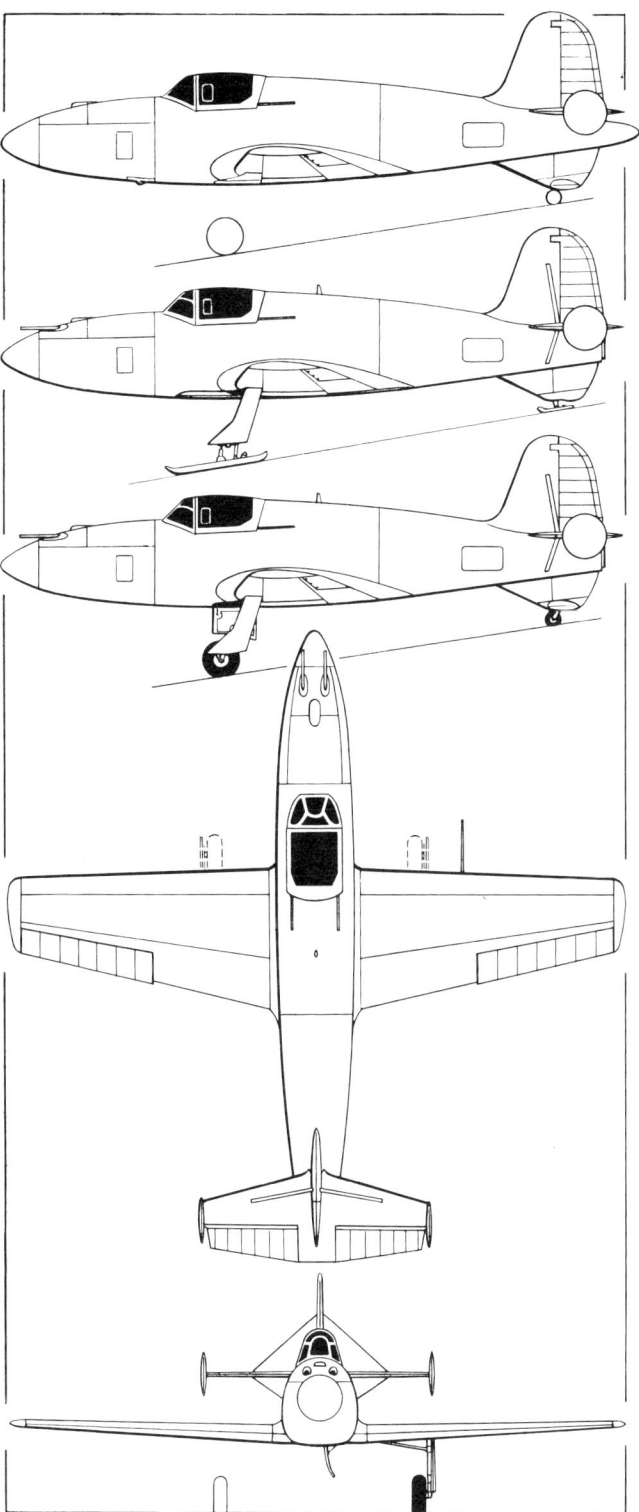

The side profile drawings above depict (top to bottom) the initial unpowered prototype BI and the powered version with both ski and wheel undercarriage

was still snow covered, the aircraft was fitted with skis which were interchangeable with the wheels. The pilot reported that control response was favourable and, as far as could be judged during the brief, low-altitude

Bereznyak-Isaev BI Cutaway Key
1 Light alloy nose cone
2 Cannon barrels
3 Gun bay/ancillaries cooling air intake
4 Gun bay support frames
5 Kerosene cylinder
6 Compressed air cylinders
7 Fuselage frame
8 Centreline radio equipment/battery bay
9 Paired 20-mm ShVAK cannon (ammunition feeds removed for clarity)
10 Ammunition tank (45 rpg)
11 Rudder pedal assembly
12 Throttle control quadrant
13 Pilot's seat/harness
14 Ventilation/clear vision panel
15 Instrument panel
16 Reflector gunsight
17 Bullet-resistant windshield
18 Starboard undercarriage leg fairing
19 Wing mainspar
20 Starboard dural-framed fabric-covered aileron
21 Flap profile
22 Canopy jettison lever
23 Single-piece aft-sliding canopy
24 Pilot's headrest
25 Unarmoured bulkhead
26 Canopy track
27 Main nitric acid cylinders
28 Main compressed air cylinder
29 Stub aerial mast
30 Aerial
31 Monocoque fuselage structure
32 Nitric acid pipes
33 Kerosene filters
34 Nitric acid filters
35 Pneumatically-controlled ON/OFF main valve
36 Direct propellant feed pipes
37 Coolant pipes
38 Injectors
39 Dushkin D-1A-1100 bi-fuel rocket motor
40 Rocket motor bearer/tailfin attachment frame
41 Tailfin structure
42 Leading edge
43 Tailplane bracing struts
44 Starboard auxiliary endplate fin
45 Aerial attachment
46 Rudder aerodynamic balance
47 Rudder structure
48 Tailplane bracing strut
49 Port elevator
50 Exhaust orifice
51 Exhaust chamber
52 Combustion chamber
53 Port auxiliary endplate fin
54 Ventral fin brace
55 Ventral fin
56 Tailwheel retraction mechanism fairing
57 Semi-retractable tailwheel
58 Alternative (fixed) ski tailskid
59 Wing root fairing
60 Dural flap structure
61 Fuselage mainframe/wing spar attachment
62 Wing ribs
63 Reinforced rib station
64 Wing rear spar
65 Aileron structure
66 Outer wing structure
67 Mainspar
68 Undercarriage leg fairing
69 Port low-pressure mainwheel tyre
70 Torque links
71 Oleo leg
72 Retraction strut
73 Pivot point
74 Port mainwheel well
75 Wheel well inner segment doors
76 Alternative ski undercarriage assembly

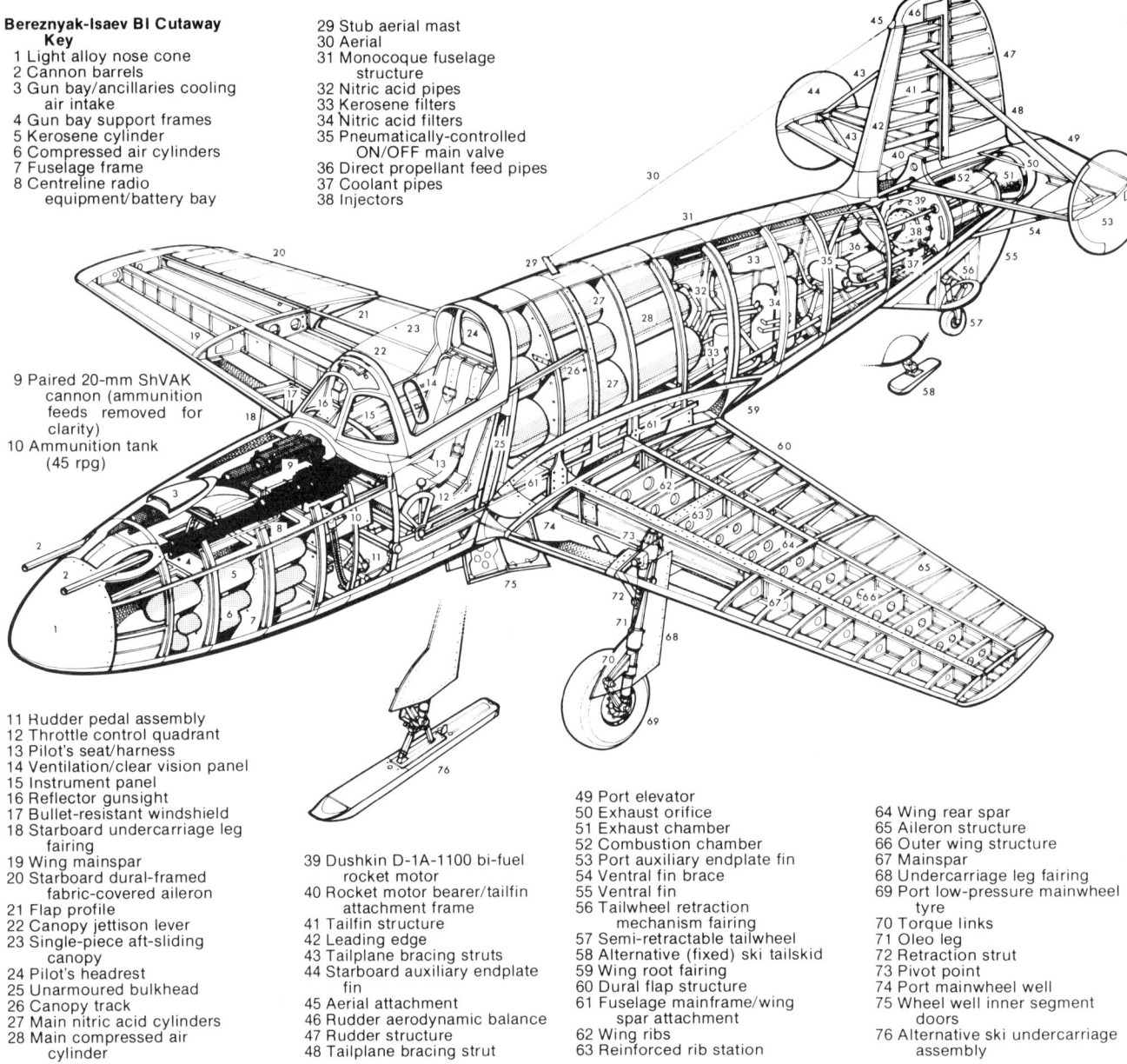

hop, the general handling characteristics of the BI in the partly-loaded condition in which it had been tested appeared acceptable. Major General Vladimir P.Fedorov, who had been assigned overall supervision of the test programme on behalf of the V-VS, together with Professor V.S.Pyshnov, who had been attached to the BI team as an adviser, then prepared a detailed schedule for the first powered flight which it was decided should take place on 15 May 1942.

The weather on the designated day proved inclement, but the crosswinds had diminished and the cloud base lifted sufficiently by early evening for the test to proceed. Accordingly, at 1900 hours, Bakhchivandzhe ignited the rocket motor of BI No 3, the tanks of which had been filled with only sufficient fuel and oxidant for some three minutes at full thrust, and at a gross weight of 2,866 lb (1 300 kg), the aircraft took-off after a run of barely 60 yards (55 m) and climbed steeply to some 2,600 ft (790 m). According to instructions, Bakhchivandzhe made no attempt to retract the skis and, as speed built up, cut the rocket motor, circling the field in a high-speed glide. Turning in for the approach and lowering the flaps, he miscalculated the sink rate, held off too long, and touched down heavily, the undercarriage collapsing but the aircraft suffering relatively minor damage. From take-off to touch-down, the flight had lasted 3 min 9 sec — the world's first genuine rocket-driven interceptor fighter had flown under power. Five months later, on 17 October, Bakhchivandzhe's flight was to be recognised with the award of the Order of Lenin, Bolkhovitinov, under whose aegis the programme had been carried through, being awarded the title of Doctor of Science.

The test programme at Koltsova now progressed slowly and by no means smoothly, delays resulting from difficulties with the temperamental rocket motor and its highly dangerous oxidant, not least of the problems being corrosion of the oxidant tanks and pipelines, and almost a year passed before a further BI airframe was fitted with its rocket motor and cleared for flight testing. In the meantime, Bakhchivandzhe was carefully exploring the performance envelope, although only a half-dozen powered flights were conducted with the BI during the 10 months following the initial test with the rocket motor operating. On the third flight, on 12 January 1943, the BI was piloted by Lt-Col Konstantin A.Gruzdev who attained a speed of 392 mph (631 km/h), but the port ski failed to extend during his landing approach. Although Gruzdev was unaware of this failure, he held the prototype level after touchdown for a considerable distance and when the port wing did drop it was cushioned by the thick snow and little damage was suffered.

On each successive flight Bakhchivandzhe attained a higher speed, and the BI team felt confident that it faced no insuperable difficulties in bringing the little warplane to operational status once the problems presented by the D-1A-1100 rocket motor had been overcome. During climbing trials, the BI attained an altitude of 16,400 ft (5 000 m) in 35 seconds and 32,810 ft (10 000 m) in 59 seconds, and it was calculated that a top speed of 600 mph (965 km/h) would be attainable at sea level, this rising to 614 mph (990 km/h) at 16,400 ft (5 000 m). On 27 March 1943, after taking-off on his seventh powered flight in the BI with the intention of performing a high-speed run at an altitude of 6,560 ft (2 000 m), Bakhchivandzhe lost his life*. Witnesses of the test flight saw a sudden puff of dense black smoke from the tailpipe and the aircraft, which it was estimated was travelling at a speed between 465 and 500 mph (750-800 km/h), appeared to develop an uncontrollable nose-down pitch and began to break up before hitting the ground a little more than a mile from the airfield.

Pending the results of an investigation into this accident, work on an initial batch of 50 BI interceptors was suspended and further flight testing, performed by Boris Kudrin, who had rejoined the team after recovering from his illness, and M.K.Baikalov, was conducted under severe restrictions, although these pilots had volunteered to duplicate the test being performed by Bakhchivandzhe which had resulted in his death. Wind tunnel testing revealed the nose-down pitch at high speeds but no obvious means of overcoming the problem presented themselves. Seven machines had been completed and some 20 additional BI fighters had attained an advanced stage in assembly at the time of Bakhchivandzhe's death, work on the partly-completed airframes being shelved and flight trials being continued in a somewhat desultory fashion with the seventh aircraft for almost two years.

Various improvements were introduced meanwhile in the D-1A-1100 rocket motor and the modified power plant was mounted in the seventh BI late in 1944, although by this time the results of the further flight

*Thirty years later, on 29 April 1973, by edict of the Praesidium of the Supreme Soviet of the USSR, Grigori Bakhchivandzhe was to receive posthumously the title of Hero of the Soviet Union and a lunar crater was to be named after him.

(Above) The second prototype BI with which pre-flight ground testing was conducted prior to a combustion chamber explosion and (below) the third BI taking-off on its first powered flight with Bakhchivandzhe at the controls

testing of the Bereznyak-Isaev fighter were of largely academic interest, the aircraft now being viewed primarily as a testbed for the rocket motor. The first flight with the improved motor installed was made by Kudrin in January 1945, but the aircraft shed its starboard ski during retraction, resulting in a forced landing and damage. On 9 March 1945, the aircraft having meanwhile been repaired, the BI was again flown by Kudrin, and during the course of this test a climb rate of 16,340 ft/min (83 m/sec) was recorded. However, this was destined to be the final flight of the BI as it coincided with the official decision to abandon the programme.

Bereznyak-Isaev BI Specification

Power Plant: One Dushkin-Isaev D-1A-1100 bi-fuel rocket motor possessing a maximum thrust of 2,425 lb (1 100 kg) for eight minutes or cruise thrust of 727 lb (330 kg) for 15 minutes. Total fuel capacity, 1,323 lb (600 kg).
Performance: Max speed (estimated), 600 mph (965 km/h) at sea level, 614 mph (990 km/h) at 16,400 ft (5 000 m); time to 16,400 ft (5 000 m), 0.58 min, to 32,810 ft (10 000 m), 0.98 min.
Weights: Empty equipped, 2,112 lb (958 kg); max loaded, 3,710 lb (1 683 kg).
Dimensions: Span, 21 ft 3⅛ in (6,48 m); length, 20 ft 11⅞ in (6,40 m); height, 6 ft 9 in (2,06 m); wing area, 75.35 sq ft (7,00 m²).
Armament: Two 20-mm Shpital'ny-Vladimirov ShVAK cannon with 45 rounds per gun.

LAVOCHKIN-GORBUNOV-GUDKOV LAGG-3

1. Cannon muzzle
2. Propeller spinner
3. VISh-61P metal variable-pitch constant-speed propeller
4. Hydraulic pitch control mechanism
5. Cowling frame
6. Hydraulic pressure tank (port segment)
7. Coolant tank (starboard segment)
8. Fuselage gun troughs
9. Klimov M-105PF 12-cylinder Vee liquid-cooled engine
10. Exhaust manifold cowling
11. Crankcase ventilation intake scoop
12. Lubricant radiator intake
13. Lubricant radiator
14. Induction air intake
15. Intake duct
16. Port mainwheel well
17. Wingroot fairing strake
18. Engine accessories
19. Forward spar carry-through
20. Lubricant tank
21. Breech of 20-mm ShVAK cannon
22. Port and starboard 7,62-mm ShKAS machine gun fairings
23. Breech of (optional) 12,7-mm UB machine gun (offset to port)
24. Starboard inner wing fuel tank (26 Imp gal/120 l capacity)
25. Starboard undercarriage pivot
26. Undercarriage position indicator
27. Starboard outer wing fuel tank (14.3 Imp gal/65 l capacity)
28. Pitot head
29. Leading-edge automatic slat
30. Automatic slat bearings
31. Starboard (upper) navigation light
32. Starboard wingtip
33. Starboard aileron
34. Aileron tab
35. Duralumin sheet split flaps
36. Rear spar
37. Welded sheet steel spar inboard/outboard connections
38. Flap actuating pushrod
39. One-piece moulded Plexiglass windscreen
40. Leather loop (canopy operation)
41. Windscreen internal frame
42. PBP-1a reflector gunsight
43. Instrument panel
44. Windscreen de-icing intake
45. Centreline fuel tank (24 Imp gal/110 l capacity)
46. Fuselage/forward spar attachment
47. Wing root rib
48. Fuselage frame/rear spar attachment
49. Rudder pedals
50. Control column
51. Pilot's seat
52. Trim handwheels
53. Main hydraulics valve
54. Aft-sliding Plexiglass canopy
55. Pilot's headrest
56. Harness
57. Back armour (9-mm)
58. Seat support frame
59. Engine coolant radiator
60. Radiator ventral bath
61. Fuselage frame
62. Electric motor (radiator outlet flap)
63. Hydraulic reservoir cylinder

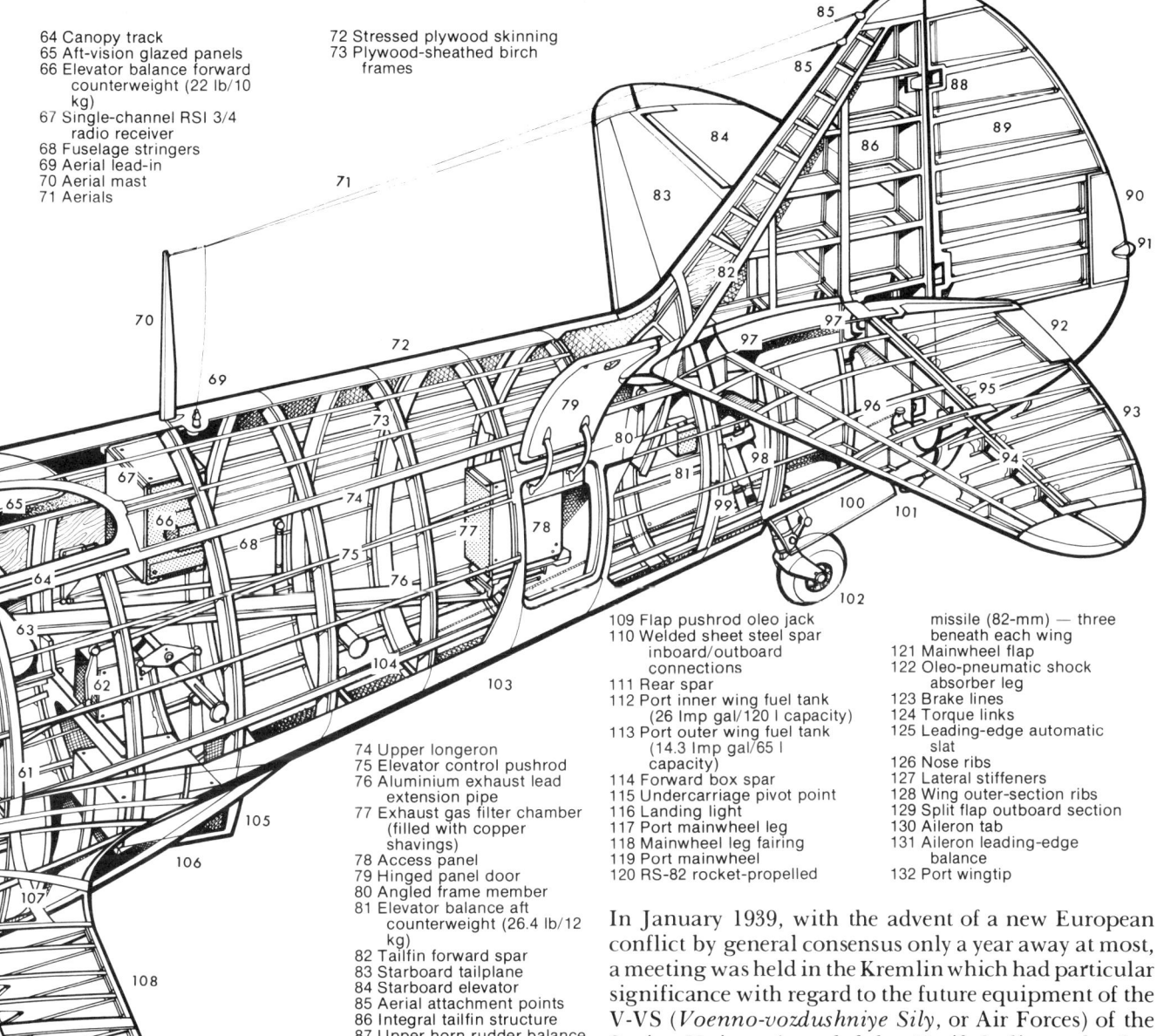

64 Canopy track
65 Aft-vision glazed panels
66 Elevator balance forward counterweight (22 lb/10 kg)
67 Single-channel RSI 3/4 radio receiver
68 Fuselage stringers
69 Aerial lead-in
70 Aerial mast
71 Aerials
72 Stressed plywood skinning
73 Plywood-sheathed birch frames
74 Upper longeron
75 Elevator control pushrod
76 Aluminium exhaust lead extension pipe
77 Exhaust gas filter chamber (filled with copper shavings)
78 Access panel
79 Hinged panel door
80 Angled frame member
81 Elevator balance aft counterweight (26.4 lb/12 kg)
82 Tailfin forward spar
83 Starboard tailplane
84 Starboard elevator
85 Aerial attachment points
86 Integral tailfin structure
87 Upper horn rudder balance (4.4 lb/2,0 kg)
88 Rudder upper hinge
89 Fabric-skinned metal-framed rudder
90 Rudder tab
91 Rear navigation light
92 Elevator tab
93 Fabric-covered metal-framed elevator
94 Elevator leading-edge balance (lead weight)
95 Elevator hinge
96 Rudder control linkage
97 Stub frame/tailplane spar attachments
98 Tailwheel oleo-pneumatic shock absorber leg
99 Hydraulic tailwheel leg actuating cylinder
100 Tailwheel door
101 Lower horn rudder balance (17.6 lb/8,0 kg)
102 Retractable tailwheel
103 Fuselage skinning
104 Rudder control cable
105 Radiator outlet
106 Ventral fairing
107 Wing root fairing
108 Split flap inboard section
109 Flap pushrod oleo jack
110 Welded sheet steel spar inboard/outboard connections
111 Rear spar
112 Port inner wing fuel tank (26 Imp gal/120 l capacity)
113 Port outer wing fuel tank (14.3 Imp gal/65 l capacity)
114 Forward box spar
115 Undercarriage pivot point
116 Landing light
117 Port mainwheel leg
118 Mainwheel leg fairing
119 Port mainwheel
120 RS-82 rocket-propelled missile (82-mm) — three beneath each wing
121 Mainwheel flap
122 Oleo-pneumatic shock absorber leg
123 Brake lines
124 Torque links
125 Leading-edge automatic slat
126 Nose ribs
127 Lateral stiffeners
128 Wing outer-section ribs
129 Split flap outboard section
130 Aileron tab
131 Aileron leading-edge balance
132 Port wingtip

In January 1939, with the advent of a new European conflict by general consensus only a year away at most, a meeting was held in the Kremlin which had particular significance with regard to the future equipment of the V-VS (*Voenno-vozdushniye Sily*, or Air Forces) of the Soviet Union. Attended by Yosif Stalin and other leading members of the Presidium, senior officers of the V-VS, representatives of the newly-constituted *Narkomavprom* (State Commissariat of the Aviation Industry) and *Narkomat Oborony* (State Commissariat for Defence), the Central Design Bureau (TsKB) and Central Institute of Aero Engine Construction (TsIAM), and the leaders of the principal aircraft design bureaux, the meeting had been convened to examine the entire spectrum of combat aircraft design, development and manufacture.

Belated appreciation of the fact that the combat equipment of the V-VS was falling behind international standards had led, in the previous year, to radical change in Soviet combat aircraft development policy. Previously, all important combat aircraft requirements had been passed either to the TsAGI (*Tsentralny aerogidrodinamichesky institut* — Central Aero- and Hydrodynamic Institute) or to the TsKB

(*Tsentralny konstruktorskoye byuro* — Central Design Bureau), each of these organisations possessing a number of individual design brigades. In an attempt to create a competitive spirit in the design of combat aircraft, the more talented of the TsAGI and TsKB brigade leaders, as well as other designers, had been given a greater degree of autonomy and encouraged to establish their own experimental design bureaux.

Among designers that had created such an OKB (*Opytno konstruktorskoye byuro* — Experimental Design Bureau) under the new system was one Semyon A.Lavochkin, who had left the GUAP (*Glavnoye upravlenie aviatsonnoi promishlennosti* — Chief Directorate of the Aviation Industry) where he had served under the Chief Engineer, Andrei N.Tupolev, in order to develop a new single-seat fighter, the project design of which he had undertaken in his spare time while with the GUAP. His OKB was joined by Vladimir P.Gorbunov and Mikhail I.Gudkov, and established in *Zavod* 301 in the Moscow suburbs, a factory originally built for the manufacture of furniture for the Palace of the Soviets and previously utilised by the OKB of A.A.Dubrovin.

The intention of Lavochkin and his associates was to develop a new 'frontal' fighter — a general-purpose tactical fighter with best combat altitude between 9,840 and 13,125 ft (3 000 and 4 000 m) — constructed primarily of wood as a means of overcoming the critical shortage of steel tube and light alloy then facing the aircraft industry. The requirement, formulated by the UV-VS (*Upravlenie Voenno-vozdushniye Sily* — Administration of the Air Force) had been circulated to more than a dozen individual OKBs on a competitive basis, and the fledgling Lavochkin OKB's project was submitted to the GUAP in the late autumn of 1938, at which time it was assigned the designation I-22*.

Among the tasks of the Kremlin meeting was the short-listing of the most promising of the 'frontal' fighter proposals and the assignment of development priorities. The submission of the Lavochkin OKB found immediate favour, both on the score of calculated performance and on the limited demands that it promised to make on materials in short supply, and thus the I-22 was one of those aircraft to which development priority was allocated.

Although aware of the weight penalty inherent in wooden construction, Semyon Lavochkin, in common with several other designers submitting proposals to meet the 'frontal' fighter requirement, believed that *delta drevesina* (delta timber) — birch *shpon*, or layers of birch strips glued cross-grained, impregnated with VIAM-B-3 (phenol-formaldehyde resin, borax and boric acid) — used in conjunction with bakelite ply (layers of birch strip bonded at 150 deg C with bakelite film) offered advantages in fighter construction that more than compensated for the weight penalty that it imposed. The *delta drevesina* had been developed by L.I.Ryzhkov, the chief engineer of a propeller blade and aircraft ski factory, and was a fire-resistant product with an appreciably greater strength than that of any untreated wood, and in the spring of 1939, the factory produced experimental spars of *delta drevesina* in order that the Lavochkin OKB could perform strength tests.

The Lavochkin team was by now expanding rapidly, having absorbed a substantial part of the design team of D.P.Grigorovich, including engineers Masolov (general layout), Strutsel (wings), Yelistan (aerodynamics) and Knyazev (stress), and during the summer of 1939, work began in *Zavod* 301 on the construction of seven prototypes of the I-22 simultaneously, the intention being to accelerate the development programme by performing both factory and state tests in parallel, the task of initial flight testing being assigned to a highly-experienced NII V-VS engineering test pilot, Aleksei I.Nikashin. By 30 March 1940, when Nikashin performed the first flight test of the new fighter — its designation of 'I-22' having meanwhile given place to that of LaGG-1 to indicate Lavochkin and his principal associates, Gorbunov and Gudkov — the rapid service phase-in of the new warplane had become a matter of such vital importance that any short cut in the time-consuming process of development to acceptable service standards was considered justified. The Russo-Finnish conflict** had revealed forcefully the inadequacy of existing V-VS fighter equipment and the introduction of a 'frontal' fighter of world standard in the shortest possible time was adjudged imperative. Thus, by the time Nikashin first flew the initial LaGG-1 prototype from the airfield adjacent to *Zavod* 301, the factory itself had already set up a production line for an initial batch of 100 fighters which it was proposed should be issued to the various experimental establishments and to service evaluation units which would then feed reports to the OKB to enable any necessary modifications or changes to be fed into the assembly line with the least possible delay and before deliveries began to the IAPs (*Istrebitel'ny aviatsionnye polki* — Fighter Aviation Regiments).

Essentially orthodox in basic configuration and designed around Vladimir Ya.Klimov's M-105P 12-cylinder Vee liquid-cooled engine derived — via a somewhat complex evolutionary process — from the Hispano-Suiza 12Y, the fighter evolved by the Lavochkin OKB featured a wooden monocoque fuselage with longerons of *delta-drevesina* and 13 plywood-sheathed birch frames, the stressed skinning being of bakelite ply ranging in thickness from 0.39 in (10 mm) forward to 0.24 in (6 mm) aft. The wooden

---

At this time, military aircraft were divided into categories and these were indicated in the aircraft designation by prefix letters, the 'I' prefix indicating Istrebitel ('Fighter', or more literally 'Destroyer'). The prefix letter was followed by a number issued to each new design in that category more or less in sequence (there were exceptions, such as I-21 assigned to a fighter developed by Sergei V.Ilyushin and flown in 1937, whereas the designation I-20 was assigned to a fighter designed by A.I.Mikoyan and M.I.Gurevich which did not fly until 1940), these numbers being assigned at the time the project was submitted to the GUAP. In 1940, this system was replaced by one utilising abbreviations of the OKB leader(s)' name(s) and affording no indication of the function of the aircraft other than fighters for which odd numbers were reserved.

**A conflict initiated on 30 November 1939 without formal declaration of war by V-VS attacks on Helsinki and Viipuri, and terminated with a Finnish capitulation on 12 March 1940.*

LaGG-3 fighters operating in the central sector in (above) the late autumn of 1941 and (right) the winter of 1941-42, and showing the rather primitive drop-shaped mass ballance weights which were applied to the top and bottom of the rudder as a temporary palliative pending a new balance system.

structure terminated forward in two heavy laminated blocks to which was bolted the tubular steel mounting for the engine, armament, ammunition and oil tanks, and accessories, the nose being covered by detachable duralumin panels. The wing, which was of standard TsAGI section with a maximum thickness of 13 per cent at 32 per cent chord, was built up on two *delta-drevesina* box spars with bakelite ply flanges, had closely-spaced ribs and featured similar skinning to that of the fuselage. It carried metal-framed fabric-covered slotted ailerons and split flaps of plain dural sheet operated by push rods on single piano hinges. The fin was built integrally with the fuselage and, like the tailplane, was of wooden construction with bakelite ply skinning, the rudder and elevators being metal framed and fabric covered.

The M-105P engine had a two-stage, two-speed mechanically-controlled blower, drove a VISh-61 three-bladed metal propeller with hydraulic pitch control and a constant-speed governor, affording 1,100 hp at 2,600 rpm for take-off and at 6,560 ft (2 000 m), and 1,050 hp at 13,120 ft (4 000 m), some 77 Imp gal (350 l) of fuel being distributed between three wing centre section tanks. The light alloy tanks were afforded a measure of protection by a sheathing of four layers of tough chord fabric impregnated with phenol-formaldehyde resin, and inert combustion gases could be introduced into the fuel tanks during combat to alleviate the fire risk. These cooled and filtered gases, consisting mainly of nitrogen and carbon monoxide, could be employed as fire suppressants for brief periods only, protracted use resulting in tank deformation.

Equipment was spartan, no gyroscopic instruments being provided; a single-channel RSI-3 radio was fitted; pilot protection was limited to a small 8-mm armour plate for head and shoulders, and armament consisted of a 23-mm Volkov-Yartsev VYa-23V cannon mounted between the cylinder banks with 80 rounds and a pair of 12,7-mm Berezin UB machine guns in the forward fuselage decking with 220 rpg.

As the test programme progressed, it was seen that, while maximum level speeds approximated in general to the values anticipated, 311 mph (500 km/h) being clocked at sea level and 373 mph (600 km/h) being attained at 16,405 ft (5 000 m), acceleration left much to be desired. Furthermore, the LaGG-1 could be out-climbed by the aged I-16, which was one of the types that it was intended to supplant; it was short on both range and ceiling; manoeuvrability was of a low order and its handling characteristics were such that it called for a very high degree of competence on the part of its pilot — a higher level of capability than was to be expected from the run-of-the-mill V-VS fighter pilot. It was soon obvious that considerable redesign and more power were necessary if the less desirable characteristics of the fighter were to be completely eradicated. As the exigencies of the times would not permit any such major redesign of the basic structure, and no alternative

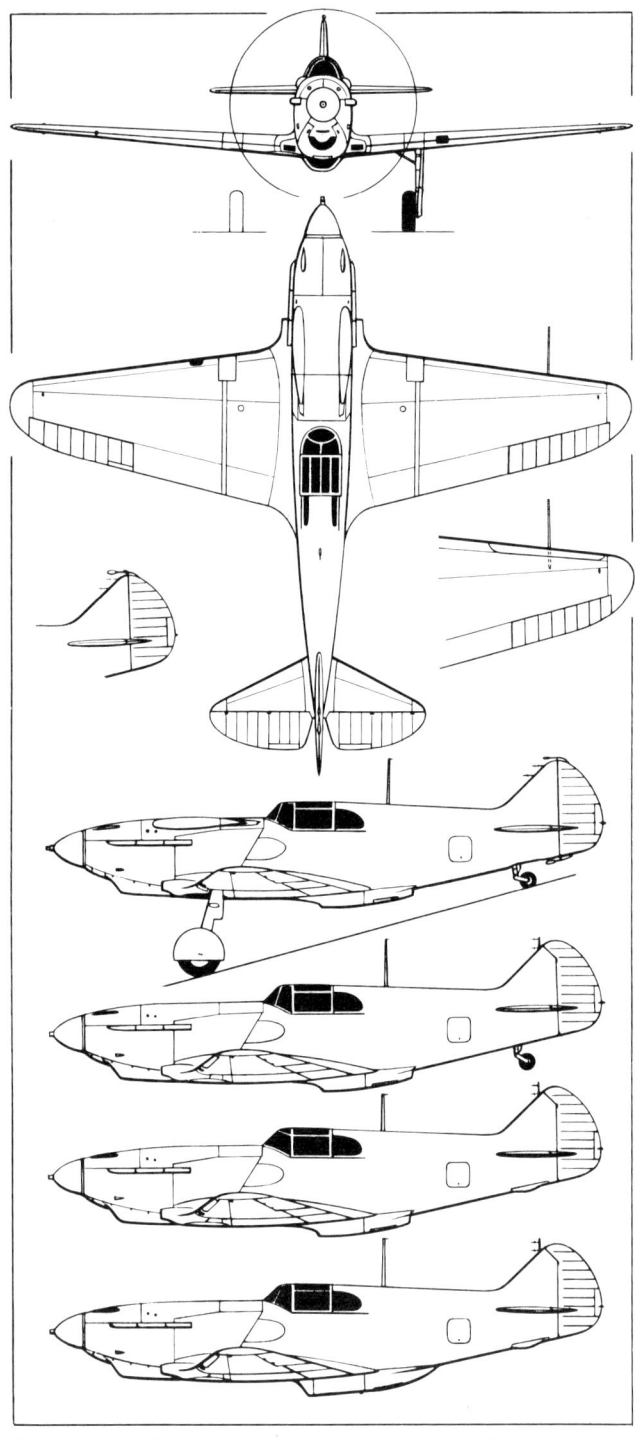

The upper three views above depict an early production LaGG 3 with 23-mm hub cannon and twin 12,7-mm cowl guns, the lefthand scrap view showing modified rudder balancing (lower weight eliminated and upper weight enlarged). The second side view shows the improved production model with 20-mm hub cannon, 7,62-mm cowl guns (either of which could be replaced by a 12,7-mm weapon), rudder weights replaced by integral tip balance and wing slats (see also righthand scrap view). The third sideview shows a refined late production model with retractable tailwheel, improved windscreen and abbreviated radio mast, and the sideview immediately above shows enlarged radiator bath

power plant immediately presented itself, the Lavochkin team had no recourse but to attempt to alleviate the more serious of the fighter's defects in a crash programme in which the NII V-VS and the TsAGI participated, the aim of the programme being to raise the LaGG-1 to at least minimum acceptable service standards without impairing production schedules.

The LaGG-1 was substantially overweight, its design team, perhaps as a result of inexperience, having produced an overly sturdy structure which was now subjected to a thoroughgoing weight analysis. Some economies were introduced as a result and a further weight saving was achieved with the replacing of the two 12,7-mm UB machine guns by two 7,62-mm ShKAS weapons, each of which was provided with 325 rounds, while the 23-mm VYa cannon gave place to a 20-mm ShVAK with 120 rounds. To render the handling characteristics more tractable, fixed slats were applied to the leading-edges of the outer wing panels — these were eventually to give place to automatic slats — while drop-shaped mass balance weights were applied to top and bottom of the rudder. A system of pendulum elevator balance weights was devised and fitted just aft of the pilot and immediately ahead of the tailwheel, the rear, heavier weight raising the elevator against the depressing action of the forward and lighter weight. Subsequently, the pendulum weights were to be eliminated and the surfaces themselves statically and dynamically balanced.

In so far as the V-VS was concerned, one of the most significant changes introduced was the redesign of the outer wing structure to permit the insertion of two 14.3 Imp gal (65 l) tanks to augment the internal fuel capacity, the inadequacy of the range of the LaGG-1 being, at that time, one of the principle causes for censure of the fighter. Provision was also made for two 22 Imp gal (100 l) external tanks, and to demonstrate the range capability of the modified aircraft, Nikashin flew the first fighter to be fitted with the revised wing a distance of 620 miles (1 000 km) in a little more than two hours. As the insufficient range of the fighter had been considered the most difficult problem to resolve, on the day after this demonstration, instructions were issued that large-scale production of the revised fighter should be initiated immediately by four additional factories — a second factory in the immediate vicinity of Moscow, a major new factory at Taganrog, *Zavod* 21 at Gor'kiy and a former agricultural machine factory (*Zavod* 153) at Novosibirsk. The modified aircraft was assigned the designation LaGG-3 and all remaining LaGG-1 airframes on the *Zavod* 301 assembly line were to be converted to what was now considered to be the definitive production standard.

Yet a further change, albeit one that could not be introduced on the production lines until late in 1941, was the replacement of the M-105P engine by the higher-boosted M-105PF (*Forsirovanny* — "Boosted"). The availability of this engine was largely the result of pressure brought by Aleksandr Yakovlev, who had been appointed a deputy to the *Narkom* (People's Com-

missar) for the Aviation Industry, Aleksei I.Shakurin, in January 1940. Anxious to obtain more power in order to alleviate some of the performance shortcomings of his own fighter, the Yak-1 (see Part Two), Yakovlev, having failed to convince Vladimir Klimov that the M-105P should be further boosted, had ordered the development of the higher-boosted engine on his own authority. The boost of the engine had been increased from 18.96 lb (1,29 *atas*) to 21.01 lb (1,43 *atas*) and the second speed of the supercharger now engaged at 8,860 ft (2 700 m) compared with 13,120 ft (4 300 m), the M-105PF being rated at 1,210 hp at 2,600 rpm for take-off and offering 1,260 hp at 2,625 ft (800 m) and 1,180 hp at 8,860 ft (2 700 m). One penalty was an increase in dry weight of 86 lb (39 kg), from 1,268 lb (575 kg) to 1,354 lb (614 kg).

Despite the tremendous impetus placed behind the improvement programme, the LaGG-3 was still a thoroughly immature warplane when it began to roll off the assembly lines early in 1941. By comparison with the similarly-powered and -armed mixed-construction Yak-1 — which, too, was by no means devoid of defects — the wooden LaGG-3 was only marginally inferior in speed and climb rate, and possessed a slightly superior range capability. It was also the sturdier of the two

(Above and below) A LaGG-3 photographed at and during trials from the Mutanchiang air base of the Japanese Army. This aircraft was flown to Manchuria by a V-VS defector in the spring of 1942, and was subsequently evaluated and flown in mock combat against its Japanese contemporaries

An example of the LaGG-3 captured by the advancing Wehrmacht in the late summer of 1941 being worked upon by Luftwaffe mechanics prior to evaluation trials. The Luftwaffe was singularly unimpressed by the performance and handling characteristics of the LaGG-3 and considered the Soviet fighter both underpowered and underarmed, and no match for such fighters as the Bf 109F, although it could absorb considerable punishment

fighters, but its poorer manoeuvrability placed it at a marked disadvantage, and its exacting handling characteristics resulted in its advent in V-VS service giving little cause for rejoicing on the part of recipient IAPs.

The hydraulic system presented its quota of difficulties; there were frequent undercarriage failures; the wheel brakes had a tendency to seize and the gun operating mechanism was unreliable. Initial conversion was accompanied by such high attrition that the acronym 'LaGG' began to take on another and more sinister connotation; V-VS pilots were suggesting that the acronym stood for *"lakirovanny garantirovanny grob"* — varnished guaranteed coffin! The Lavochkin fighter was openly referred to as a "mortician's mate"; an aircraft whose intentions towards its pilots were no more benevolent than would be those of the *Luftwaffe* that the V-VS anticipated soon finding itself opposing.

This censure of the LaGG-3 was not without some justification as the fighter revealed much evidence of the haste with which it had been tested and committed to production. Any but a highly-experienced pilot found it a difficult machine to fly. It was overweight, underpowered and unforgiving; it was prone to developing an unheralded and vicious spin from a steep banking turn; it tended to nose-up during an approach and stall at the least provocation; its undercarriage was weak and view from the cockpit was inadequate.

These defects were compounded by the inadequacy of the conversion training afforded its pilots, who had, for the most part, previously flown the forgiving and extraordinarily manoeuvrable I-152 biplane. To service pilots, the performance of the new fighter appeared markedly inferior to that predicted, although, in truth, this was not the result of overly-optimistic calculations on the part of the Lavochkin OKB. Apart from poor manufacturing standards resulting from the inadequacies of the hurriedly-recruited and ill-trained personnel largely manning the rapidly expanding aircraft industry which manifested themselves in the form of ill-fitting panels and poor surface finishes, with an understandable effect on performance, the inadequately-trained pilots had a tendency to fly at full throttle with the air intakes fully open at a penalty of 6-9 mph (10-15 km/h), and most pilots flew with their cockpit canopies open, reducing the unfortunate warplane's performance by another 12-15 mph (20-25 km/h). Their reluctance to close the hood in flight was understandable in that it lacked provision for jettisoning and was difficult to open in an emergency, while the Plexiglass from which it was manufactured was almost as opaque as bottle glass, seriously impairing vision when the hood was closed. One *eskadril* leader was to go on record as commenting that, with a canopy such as that of the LaGG-3, the first that he would know of the proximity of an enemy aircraft would be the sound of its bullets hammering on the Plexiglass! Later, after the commencement of the German invasion, the performance problem was to be further aggravated by the application of thick layers of camouflage paint at the cost of some 6 mph (10 km/h), while RS-82 rocket missiles hung beneath the wings were to pare off some 12 mph (20 km/h) more.

Production tempo built up rapidly — by 30 June 1941, eight days after the commencement of the *Wehrmacht* assault, 322 LaGG-3s had been completed, and during the remaining six months of the year, the daily output was to average 12.7 aircraft to provide a total of 2,141 aircraft between July and December, more than double the quantity of Yak-1s delivered over the same period. As more IAPs converted to the LaGG-3, a special team was formed under the leadership of Lavochkin's deputy, S.M.Alekseyev, for direct liaison between the operational IAPs and the factories, but so serious had the situation become towards the end of 1941, that Semyon Lavochkin found it necessary to personally tour the LaGG-3 bases in order to investigate the shortcomings of his progeny at first hand.

The LaGG-3 IAPs were suffering inordinate losses in combat and their morale was at low ebb in consequence, all blame being levelled at their equipment. Thus, Lavochkin was accompanied by two of the leading test pilots of the NII V-VS, Konstantin Gruzdev and Aleksei Grinchik, both of whom had flown the

LaGG-3 operationally and with success, and whose task it was to demonstrate to frontline pilots the most effective methods of flying the Lavochkin fighter in combat. Lt.Col.Gruzdev, who had claimed some 20 'kills' while flying the LaGG-3 during the first months of the conflict, had evolved the technique of using 10-15 deg of flap to tighten the fighter's turn, while Grinchik possessed the unusual distinction of having shot down an enemy fighter while *gliding*! On this occasion, his LaGG-3 had taken a direct hit in the engine and while gliding down for a forced landing was continuously under attack from Bf 109s. The pilot of one of these *Luftwaffe* fighters had the misfortune to miscalculate a firing pass and place his aircraft squarely in Grinchik's gunsight.

Some V-VS pilots *had* flown the LaGG-3 with noteworthy success. V.I. Popkov, the V-VS's 15th ranking 'ace', had gained his first 'kills' while flying the LaGG-3, as did also P.Golovachev, V.Zaitsev, S.Lugansky and N.Skomorokhov, who, like Popkov, were to be twice awarded the title of Hero of the Soviet Union. Another Hero of the Soviet Union, Capt.G.A.Grigoryev, gained 15 'kills' during the first six months of the war with the LaGG-3, and on 21 March 1942, five LaGG-3s of the 5 Guards IAP led by Capt. V.Yefremov were to encounter a force of 30 *Luftwaffe* aircraft and destroy seven of them without loss. There were to be many occasions, also, when the LaGG-3 was to display its extraordinary sturdiness in no uncertain fashion, such as that in the summer of 1942, when the tail of the LaGG-3 flown by Guards Sen.Lt.I.Bikmykhametov struck the wing of a Bf 109 with such force that the German fighter crashed but the Lavochkin fighter returned to its base displaying little damage.

These were, however, exceptionally capable pilots flying for the most part with crack IAPs, and the average V-VS pilot mounted on the LaGG-3 did not

The Finnish air arm, Ilmavoimat, acquired three examples of the LaGG-3 and, surprisingly, employed these aircraft operationally, two of them, LG-1 and LG-3, being illustrated below. These served primarily in the tactical reconnaissance role (1943-44) with LeLv 32 and (1945) HLeLv 11. Finnish pilots were critical of the LaGG-3's acceleration and disliked its tendency to enter a spin from a tight turn

This example of the LaGG-3 (LG-1) had a starboard 12,7-mm cowl gun, no slats and a tip rudder balance only

The example of the LaGG-3 (LG-3) utilised by the Finnish air arm and illustrated below and above right was apparently a late production example with a single ShKAS machine gun over the engine (to port), a horn-balanced rudder and an enlarged radiator bath. The leading-edge slats may just be seen in the front view

consider himself fortunate. While the introduction of the M-105PF engine from late 1941 was welcomed, enabling climbing time to 16,405 ft (5 000 m) to be reduced from 6.2 to 5.6 minutes, the LaGG-3 was destined to remain unpopular with its pilots, even after they had mastered its idiosyncrasies, and it was tacitly admitted to be inferior to the Messerschmitt Bf 109 in most respects and totally outclassed by the Focke-Wulf Fw 190. An improved windscreen embodying 55-mm armourglass and a canopy of acceptably-clear Plexiglass had been introduced on the LaGG-3 by late 1941; a reconnaissance variant had been evolved with a semi-automatic AFA-I camera; additional instrumentation, landing lights and an RSI-4 radio were fitted for the nocturnal intercept role, and various attempts were made to improve the fighter's armament, which was the subject of much criticism, but in so far as changes that would have affected deliveries were concerned, the *Narkomavprom* insisted that the factories adhere religiously to its slogan "Do not touch the production line!" Thus, many of the requests to make changes submitted by the Lavochkin OKB went unheeded.

With regard to the armament of the LaGG-3, the majority of fighters of this type standardised on the hub-mounted ShVAK cannon, which had a muzzle velocity of 2,625 ft/sec (800 m/sec) and a fire rate of 800 rpm, and the paired 7,62-mm ShKAS machine guns, these having a muzzle velocity of 2,705 ft/sec (824 m/sec) and a fire rate of 1,800 rpm. This armament was used in conjunction with a PBP-1a lens-type reflector sight, a rather rudimentary affair with two deflection rings — one for 124 mph (200 km/h) and the other for 186 mph (300 km/h) — but unable to afford any fine degree of deflection and necessitating firing full fore and aft of the target in combat.

Repeated requests were received from the frontline that the 12,7-mm UB machine gun as mounted in the original LaGG-1 be reinstated despite the weight penalty that this invoked. With a muzzle velocity of 2,820 ft/sec (860 m/sec) and a fire rate of 1,000 rpm, the UB, or *Universalny Berezin*, was an extremely reliable weapon with particularly good ballistic characteristics and was widely considered to be as effective as the 20-mm ShVAK cannon. Provision was therefore made for the replacement of either port or starboard ShKAS with the larger-calibre weapon over the engine, the UB being provided with 220 rounds, and in some cases both the ShKAS guns were replaced by UBs.

As the LaGG-3 was increasingly employed in the low-level close-support and ground attack role, for which its ability to absorb considerable battle damage and remain airborne rendered it particularly well suited, the 23-mm VYa-23V cannon frequently replaced the hub-mounted ShVAK, the larger cannon, which was claimed to be capable of penetrating armour of up to one inch (25 mm) thickness, having a muzzle velocity of 2,953 ft/sec (900 m/sec) and a fire rate of 600 rpm. Some LaGG-3s were modified by forward maintenance units to mount an armament of five UB machine guns, two of these being carried beneath the wings, and six RS-82 rocket projectiles were frequently carried.

Alternative external stores loads included the previously-mentioned pair of 25 Imp gal (100 l) auxiliary tanks, two 110-lb (50-kg) and two 55-lb (25-kg) bombs, or two 220-lb (100-kg) bombs.

In view of its admitted deficiencies, the *Narkomavprom* issued a directive that the LaGG-3 should be withdrawn from the assembly lines as soon as a successor could take its place without impeding the flow of combat aircraft to the hard-pressed IAPs. The main Lavochkin OKB had been evacuated from Moscow and re-established in *Zavod* 21 at Gor'kiy, on the Volga to the east of Moscow, during the autumn of 1941, and the Taganrog factory had been evacuated to Tbilisi, in Georgia, where production of the LaGG-3 was to continue into the summer of 1942, the Novosibirsk plant (*Zavod* 153) being ordered to convert to Yak-1 production as rapidly as the LaGG-3 could be phased out. At one time, a Yak-1 assembly line was to be operating in *Zavod* 153 alongside a LaGG-3 line*.

Mikhail Gudkhov, who remained behind at the Moscow factory with a nucleus of design staff when the main OKB was transferred to Gor'kiy, supervised the completion of three prototypes of the so-called LaGG-3K-37, a version intended specifically for the anti-armour role and fitted with a gas-operated Shpital'ny-Komaritsky 37-mm cannon which replaced the ShVAK between the cylinder banks of the M-105P engine and necessitated repositioning of the pilot's cockpit. In the event, this particular weapon was to be discontinued in favour of the competitive Nudelmann-Suranov recoil-operated cannon of similar calibre, and development of the LaGG-3K-37 was abandoned when German forces pushed close to the boundary of the airfield adjacent to the factory.

At this time, Gudkhov was also working on the mating of the LaGG-3 airframe with the only immediately available alternative power plant to the M-105P of suitable power, the 1,540 hp Shvetsov M-82 14-cylinder radial air-cooled engine, this being taken from the Sukhoi Su-2 *shturmovik*, complete with engine bearers, cowling and propeller. Known variously as the LaGG-3/M-82 and Gu-82, two prototypes were constructed, but only one of these had been completed and was still awaiting flight testing when, in October 1941, the factory was hurriedly evacuated. In consequence, Gudkhov's M-82-powered LaGG-3 was not flown until the following summer, by which time a similarly-powered derivative of the LaGG-3 evolved in parallel at the Tbilisi factory by Semyon Lavochkin and Engineer Valedinsky from Arkadii D. Shvetsov's bureau had been flying successfully for some three months and had been ordered into production (see La-5).

Although viewed somewhat unfavourably in official circles by early 1942, owing to what were considered to be repeated failure to eradicate the remaining shortcomings of the LaGG-3, and left with only a small proportion of his original design team, which,

---

*Aleksandr Yakovlev was later to recall that when he arrived at the Novosibirsk factory, it was littered with incomplete LaGG-3s as was also the adjoining airfield, some not being discovered until the snow melted in the following spring.

meanwhile, had been transferred to Tbilisi, Semyon Lavochkin still sought means of improving the basic fighter in less drastic a fashion than redesigning the aircraft to take an air-cooled radial engine and despite the official pronouncement that the LaGG-3 was to be withdrawn from production at the earliest opportunity.

Thus, in parallel with work on the M-82 radial-engined variant, the OKB worked on the so-called LaGG-3 *Dubler* (literally "Understudy"), which was essentially a standard airframe powered by an M-105PF-2, and the *oblechenny* (lightened) LaGG-3. The M-105PF-2 operated at higher revs than the PF-1 version of the engine that had been standardised for the LaGG-3, and suffered some 30 per cent reduction in TBO (Time Between Overhauls) in consequence, producing 1,244 hp at 2,700 rpm for take-off and 1,300 hp at 2,625 ft (800 m). Flight testing of the *Dubler* was never completed, although a maximum speed of 384 mph (618 km/h) was anticipated at 11,155 ft (3 400 m). No greater success was achieved with the lightened version of the LaGG-3 in which both structure and equipment were revised to save more than 600 lb (272 kg), the loaded weight being reduced to 6,316 lb (2 865 kg). Armament was reduced to a hub-mounted lightweight B-20 (MP-20) 20-mm cannon and a single UB machine gun. Performance did not display a sufficient advance to warrant further development.

Serious consideration was given to the possibility of utilising the new Klimov M-107A engine to provide the additional power required by the LaGG-3, and a pre-production example of this power plant was installed in a LaGG-3 airframe during the summer of 1942 at Tbilisi, flight testing being conducted by G.Mishchenko. Rated at 1,650 hp at 5,905 ft (1 800 m) and 1,430 hp at 14,928 ft (4 550 m), the M-107A bid fair to endow the Lavochkin fighter with an outstanding performance but, unfortunately, was at an early stage in its development and suffering numerous teething troubles. The M-107A-powered LaGG-3 was flown a total of 33 times, but its test pilot, Mishchenko, subsequently remarked that 33 take-offs had merely produced 33 forced landings! Yet another proposal for increasing the performance of the LaGG-3 that was to fall by the wayside was one calling for the application of a small Bocharev ramjet for use as an auxiliary booster. Although some ground testing was conducted, it was eventually realised that the drag of the ramjet installation would, when the unit was not operating, impose an unacceptable penalty on the fighter's performance.

The LaGG-3's *Luftwaffe* opponents were generally of the opinion that the fighter was underpowered and under-armed, and that the serious weak spots were its coolant radiator and wing tanks. The Finns acquired three captured examples of the LaGG-3 from the *Luftwaffe* which they not only evaluated but placed in service with LeLv-3 for tactical reconnaissance missions, and on one occasion a Finnish-flown LaGG-3 actually encountered a LaGG-3 of the V-VS in combat. A protracted dogfight followed in which neither pilot could establish an ascendancy over the other, the conflict being broken off only when the Finnish pilot's ShVAK cannon jammed. Finnish pilots were said to have felt that the Lavochkin fighter was, in some indefinable way, "unfinished". They commended its stability in horizontal flight, criticised its acceleration and tendency to enter a spin from a tight turn, but stressed the fact that their Hawk 75As experienced no great difficulty in combating the LaGG-3 when flown by an average V-VS pilot, despite the superior speed performance of the Soviet fighter, and the Finns considered the Lavochkin to be completely outclassed by the Messerschmitt Bf 109G.

The Japanese, too, had an opportunity to evaluate the LaGG-3 when, in the spring of 1942, a V-VS pilot whose unit had just converted to the fighter from the I-16, defected to Manchuria and made a wheels-up landing in a ploughed field near Chiamus. On 27 September 1942, after repairs had been effected, evaluation began under the supervision of Major Yamamoto from the Army Air Test Centre. Although the Japanese test pilots' remarks concerning the manoeuvrability of the LaGG-3 were scathing, they were more impressed by the capabilities of the Soviet fighter than were their Finnish contemporaries.

By late-summer of 1942, the last of 6,528 LaGG-3 fighters had been delivered to the V-VS — an extraordinarily large number of aircraft in view of the fact that production had not begun to gain momentum until the summer of the previous year and indicative of the prodigious effort that had been placed behind the manufacturing programme — and a substantial number of additional airframes were being adapted to take the M-82 air-cooled radial engine as the La-5; an adaptation that was to prove remarkably more successful than had its progenitor.

LaGG-3 Specification
Power Plant: One Klimov M-105PF-1 12-cylinder Vee liquid-cooled engine rated at 1,210 hp at 2,600 rpm for take-off, 1,260 hp at 2,700 rpm at 2,625 ft (800 m) and 1,180 hp at 2,700 rpm at 8,860 ft (2 700 m), driving a 9 ft 10 in (3,00 m) diam VISh-61 three-blade constant-speed metal propeller. Total fuel capacity of 105.5 Imp gal (480 l) distributed between five tanks.
Performance: Max speed, 307 mph (495 km/h) at sea level, 322 mph (518 km/h) at 3,280 ft (1 000 m), 332 mph (535 km/h) at 6,560 ft (2 000 m), 342 mph (550 km/h) at 9,840 ft (3 000 m), 354 mph (570 km/h) at 13,120 ft (4 000 m), 349 mph (562 km/h) at 16,400 ft (5 000 m), 343 mph (552 km/h) at 19,685 ft (6 000 m); max continuous cruise, 283 mph (455 km/h); range (internal fuel), 345 mls (556 km), (with two 22 Imp gal/100 l external tanks), 435 mls (700 km); time to 16,400 ft (5 000 m), 5.85 min; service ceil, 31,495 ft (9,600 m).
Weights: Empty equipped, 5,776 lb (2 620 kg); normal loaded, 6,944 lb (3 150 kg); max loaded, 7,452 lb (3 380 kg).
Dimensions: Span, 32 ft 1⅞ in (9,80 m); length, 28 ft 11 in (8,81 m); height, 14 ft 5¼ in (4,40 m); wing area, 188.37 sq ft (17,50 m²).
Armament: One 20-mm Shpital'ny-Vladimirov ShVAK cannon with 120 rounds and two 7,62-mm Shpital'ny-Komaritsky ShKAS machine guns with 325 rpg. Alternative external loads: six 82-mm RS-82 rockets, two 110-lb (50-kg) and two 55-lb (25-kg) bombs, or two 220-lb (100-kg) bombs.

LAVOCHKIN LA-5

In the spring of 1942, Semyon A. Lavochkin was, if not in disgrace, certainly in official disfavour as a result of the lack of success that had attended his repeated attempts to eradicate what had proved to be fundamental shortcomings in his LaGG-3 fighter. His OKB had been reduced to a bare nucleus and was no more than a "guest" of the Tbilisi factory to which it had been transferred, while the factories that had manufactured the LaGG-3 had been committed to the progeny of other designers. Yet, barely more than a year later, on 21 June 1943, Lavochkin was to be recipient of the coveted title of Hero of Socialist Labour and his prestige as a fighter designer was to be at its zenith; an extraordinary metamorphosis but one no more dramatic than the transformation of the capabilities of his fighter that was to bring about so radical a change in Lavochkin's circumstances. Indeed, the substitution of an air-cooled radial power plant for the liquid-cooled inline engine for which the Lavochkin fighter had been designed was, fortuitously, to result in the creation of one of the outstanding combat aircraft of World War II and, incidentally, the last single-seat fighter of classic wooden construction to see large-scale production and service.

The mating of a radial engine with a single-seat fighter airframe designed expressly for an inline power plant was to be by no means uncommon during World War II, but without major redesign of fundamental components, few such marital unions were to enjoy sufficient success to warrant series production. A noteworthy exception, however, was provided by the rebirth of the inline-engined LaGG-3 as the radial-engined La-5. The adaptation of all existing production inline-engined single-seat fighter airframes to take a radial power plant had been pursued as an official directive from the summer of 1941 when a suitable radial engine attained production status. The primary purpose of the programme was that of safeguarding against any shortfall in the delivery of inline units for which the fighters had been conceived, and, in due course, the AM-35A-powered MiG-3 and the M-105P-engined Yak-7B and LaGG-3 were all experimentally re-engined, the power plant prompting this programme being the 14-cylinder two-row M-82 radial, which, developed by Arkadii D. Shvetsov's bureau, had successfully completed its State Acceptance Trials and had been placed in production in May 1941.

The M-82 owed much to the Wright Cyclone 14 but had a shorter stroke (155 mm), a smaller swept volume (41,2 l), a higher compression ratio (1 : 7) and smaller overall dimensions. With a two-speed supercharger, its nominal maximum continuous power was 1,540 hp at 6,725 ft (2 050 m), 1,700 hp being available for take-off at 2,400 rpm and dry weight being 1,874 lb (850 kg). The mating of the M-82, with its diameter of 47.48 in (1 260 mm), with the LaGG-3's cross section intended to cater

Early production examples of the La-5 (above left and below) utilised modified LaGG-3 airframes from the Gor'kiy and Tbilisi assembly lines, new production airframes differing primarily in having a cut-down rear fuselage for improved aft vision. The first conversions were flown operationally within a few weeks of leaving the factory

The initial production La-5, illustrated above and right, could be distinguished from the late La-5FN primarily by the supercharger air intake trunk fairing, which, on the later model, was extended to the lip of the cowling, The debut of the La-5 on the Stalingrad front came as something of a surprise to the Luftwaffe, which, while unimpressed by the new fighter's firepower, developed respect for its manoeuvrability

for the 30.59-in (77,7-mm) width of the M-105 was no simple task, and was one complicated by the differing thrust lines of the two power plants and the substantially greater weight of the radial engine which was 551 lb (250 kg) more than that of the inline engine that it was intended to supplant. The CG was disturbed further by the elimination of the ventral radiator bath and trunking, rendered superfluous by the air-cooled engine and remained sufficiently critical to permit installation of only the minimum acceptable armament, this comprising two belt-fed gas-operated 20-mm ShVAK cannon mounted in the forward fuselage ahead of the cockpit with 200 rpg.

An extremely close fitting, tapered cowling was adopted, this owing much to the work of Engineer Valedinsky from Arkadii Shvetsov's bureau, and embodied adjustable louvres to control the flow of cooling air. Front and rear fans were provided for warm weather operation, the exhaust pipes were clustered together horizontally on each side of the forward fuselage, affording some measure of thrust augmentation, and a VISh-105V three-blade controllable-pitch propeller was used, the hub incorporating a Huckstype starter dog for use when compressed air was not available for the self-starter.

The prototype M-82 conversion of a LaGG-3 airframe was completed in the small experimental shop attached to Lavochkin's OKB at the Tbilisi factory in December 1941, barely two months after the commencement of design studies, but flight testing could not be initiated until the following March owing to a combination of circumstances. Inclement weather and cooling difficulties with the M-82 engine during ground running were compounded by the uncooperative attitude of the factory director, who, aware of the disfavour in which Lavochkin was held, was anxious not to compromise himself. Flight trials finally began, however, with the OKB's test pilot,

Lavochkin La-5FN Cutaway Key

1. Hucks-type starter dog
2. Spinner
3. Propeller balance
4. Controllable frontal intake louvres
5. VISh-105V metal controllable-pitch three-bladed propeller
6. Nose ring profile
7. Intake centrebody
8. ShVAK cannon port
9. Supercharger air intake
10. Supercharger intake trunk fairing
11. Blast tube
12. Shvetsov M-82FN 14-cylinder two-row radial
13. Cowling ring
14. Cowling panel hinge line
15. Exhaust pipes
16. Exhaust outlet cluster (seven per side)
17. Outlet cover panel
18. Engine accessories
19. Mainspar/fuselage attachment
20. Ammunition tanks (200 rpg)
21. Link and cartridge ejection chutes
22. Engine bearer upper support bracket
23. Cannon breech fairing
24. Paired 20-mm ShVAK cannon
25. Supercharger intake trunking
26. Stressed bakelite-ply skinning
27. Automatic leading-edge slat (obliquely-operated)
28. Pitot head
29. Starboard navigation light
30. Wingtip
31. Dural-framed fabric-covered aileron
32. Aileron trim tab
33. Armourglass windscreen (55-mm)
34. PBP-1a reflector gunsight
35. Cockpit air
36. Control column
37. Outlet louvres
38. Rudder pedal assembly
39. Underfloor control linkage
40. Rear spar/fuselage attachment
41. Rudder and elevator trim handwheels
42. Seat height adjustment
43. Boost controls
44. Seat harness
45. Pilot's seat
46. Throttle quadrant
47. Hydraulics main valve
48. Aft-sliding cockpit canopy
49. Fixed aft transparent cockpit fairing
50. Armourglass screen (75-mm)
51. Canopy track
52. RSI-4 HF R/T installation
53. Radio equipment shelf
54. Dural fuselage side panels
55. Control cables
56. Plywood-sheathed birch frames with triangular-section wooden stringers
57. Stressed bakelite-ply skinning
58. Accumulator
59. Accumulator access panel
60. Tailfin frontspar attachment
61. Aerial mast
62. Radio aerials
63. Starboard tailplane
64. Elevator hinge
65. Dural-framed fabric-covered elevator
66. Tailfin leading edge
67. Tailfin wooden structure (plywood skinning)
68. Aerial stub
69. Rudder balance
70. Rudder upper hinge
71. Dural-framed fabric-covered rudder
72. Rudder trim tab
73. Rear navigation light
74. Rudder centre hinge
75. Elevator control lever
76. Tailplane/fuselage attachment
77. Rudder control lever
78. Elevator trim tab
79. Dural-framed fabric-covered elevator
80. Wooden two-spar tailplane structure (plywood skinning)
81. Tailwheel doors
82. Aft-retracting tailwheel (usually locked in extended position)
83. Tailwheel leg
84. Tailwheel shock strut
85. Retraction mechanism
86. Stressed bakelite-ply skinning
87. Retractable access step
88. Wing root fillet
89. Dural-skinned flap construction
90. Aileron tab
91. Dural-framed fabric-covered aileron
92. Wingtip
93. Port navigation light
94. Leading-edge automatic slat (obliquely operated)
95. Outboard ribs

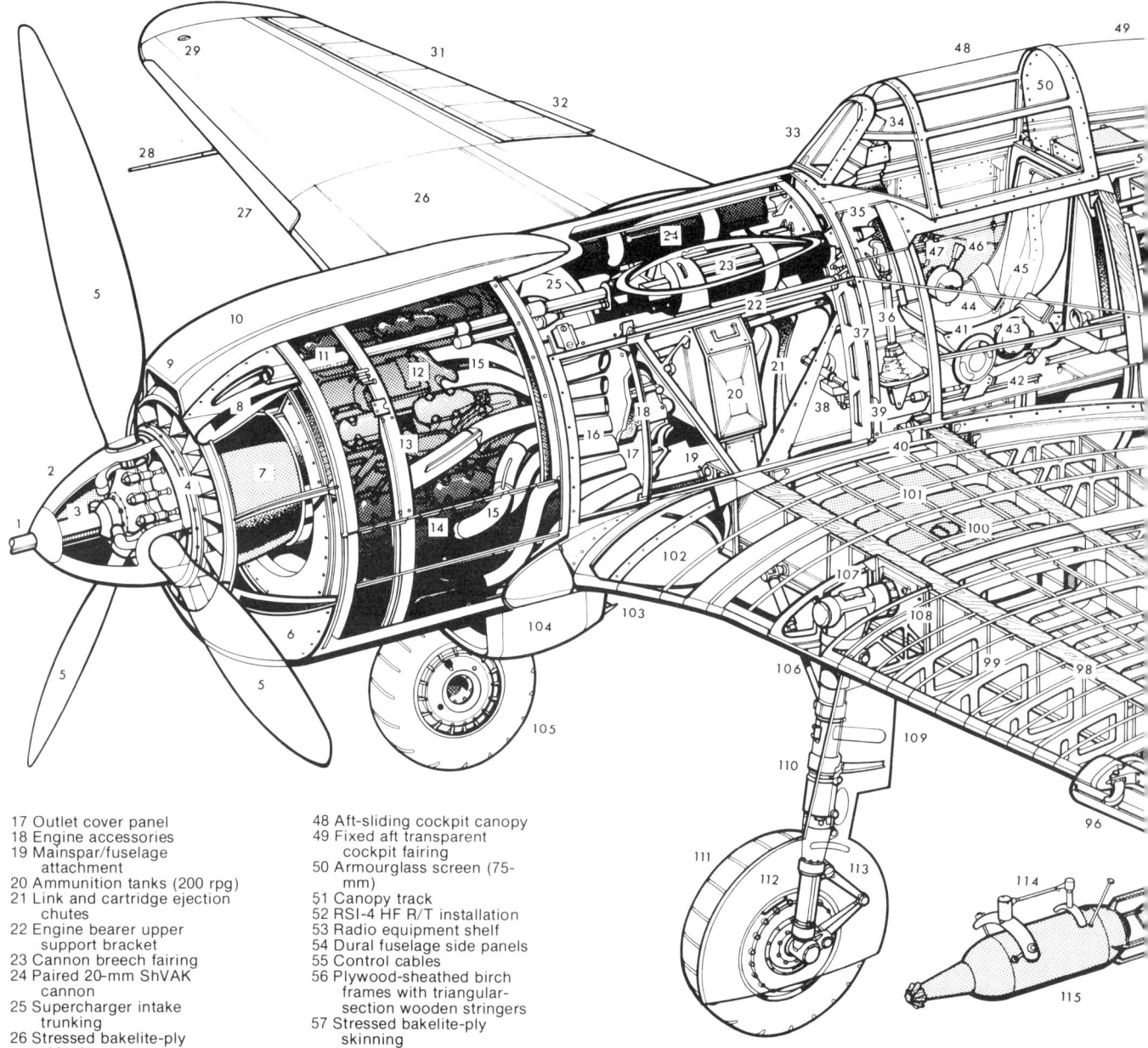

20

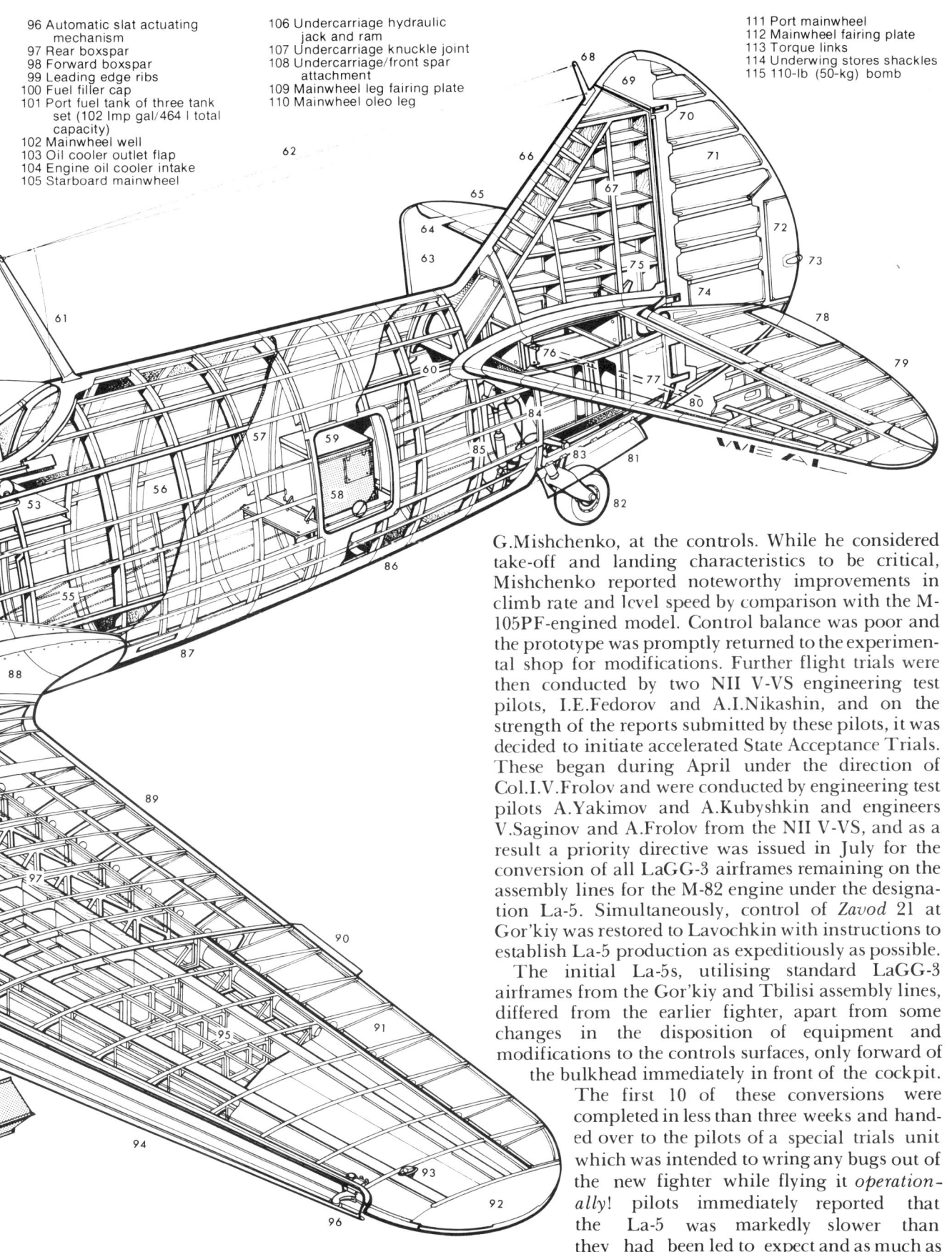

96 Automatic slat actuating mechanism
97 Rear boxspar
98 Forward boxspar
99 Leading edge ribs
100 Fuel filler cap
101 Port fuel tank of three tank set (102 Imp gal/464 l total capacity)
102 Mainwheel well
103 Oil cooler outlet flap
104 Engine oil cooler intake
105 Starboard mainwheel
106 Undercarriage hydraulic jack and ram
107 Undercarriage knuckle joint
108 Undercarriage/front spar attachment
109 Mainwheel leg fairing plate
110 Mainwheel oleo leg
111 Port mainwheel
112 Mainwheel fairing plate
113 Torque links
114 Underwing stores shackles
115 110-lb (50-kg) bomb

G.Mishchenko, at the controls. While he considered take-off and landing characteristics to be critical, Mishchenko reported noteworthy improvements in climb rate and level speed by comparison with the M-105PF-engined model. Control balance was poor and the prototype was promptly returned to the experimental shop for modifications. Further flight trials were then conducted by two NII V-VS engineering test pilots, I.E.Fedorov and A.I.Nikashin, and on the strength of the reports submitted by these pilots, it was decided to initiate accelerated State Acceptance Trials. These began during April under the direction of Col.I.V.Frolov and were conducted by engineering test pilots A.Yakimov and A.Kubyshkin and engineers V.Saginov and A.Frolov from the NII V-VS, and as a result a priority directive was issued in July for the conversion of all LaGG-3 airframes remaining on the assembly lines for the M-82 engine under the designation La-5. Simultaneously, control of *Zavod* 21 at Gor'kiy was restored to Lavochkin with instructions to establish La-5 production as expeditiously as possible.

The initial La-5s, utilising standard LaGG-3 airframes from the Gor'kiy and Tbilisi assembly lines, differed from the earlier fighter, apart from some changes in the disposition of equipment and modifications to the controls surfaces, only forward of the bulkhead immediately in front of the cockpit.

The first 10 of these conversions were completed in less than three weeks and handed over to the pilots of a special trials unit which was intended to wring any bugs out of the new fighter while flying it *operationally*! pilots immediately reported that the La-5 was markedly slower than they had been led to expect and as much as

(Above) An early example of the La-5UTI two-seater converted on the La-5F assembly line, and (foot of page) an La-5F brought down by groundfire, the pilot having made a forced landing behind the German lines

31 mph (50 km/h) slower at 19,685 ft (6 000 m). This performance shortfall was confirmed by pilots of the State Acceptance Commission and Lavochkin was promptly summoned to the Kremlin to explain to Stalin and Malenkov why the fighter was not fulfilling its earlier promise. A report by a TsAGI investigation team that had been sent to the factory indicated that the primary reason for the loss in performance was drag from the ill-fitting handmade engine cowling and in admonishing Lavochkin, Stalin told him that the responsibility for "looking after the finish" of his fighters was his alone. "Things must be improved at once!" declared Stalin, Malenkov adding that *his* (Lavochkin's) performance would in future be scrutinised closely!

Lavochkin's troubles were by no means over, however, for, in the meantime, two of the initial batch of La-5s had crashed as a result of losing wings — one during a shallow dive and the other during a landing approach — both pilots being killed. These crashes followed complaints of excessive vibration in cruising flight. Furthermore, when the guns were fired,

vibration was so strong that the gunsight was rendered useless. All La-5s were grounded and an emergency investigation was conducted by factory, TsAGI and NII V-VS personnel. It was ascertained that the wing failures had resulted from the holes for the bolts attaching the wing centre section to the outer panels having been too small and, as a result, the bolts being hammered in, weakening the structure. Vibration in cruising flight was traced to the incorrect balancing of the propeller blades and vibration during gun firing was resolved by some redesign of the cannon mounting to incorporate increased damping.

With these modifications, the La-5 was cleared for service testing and, in September 1942, a hastily-formed trials regiment was deployed to an airfield in the vicinity of Stalingrad where the *Wehrmacht* was concentrating on the capture of the city's 30-mile (48-km) perimeter astride the Volga and where what was to become a tremendous battle of attrition had begun late in the previous month. The new fighter received immediate acclamation. Retaining the sturdiness that had characterised the LaGG-3 but proving extraordinarily manoeuvrable and in this respect the master of any aircraft by which it was opposed, the La-5 was a superlative low-to-medium altitude superiority fighter, excelling in close-in high-g manoeuvring style of combat. Control was sensitive; climb and dive qualities were good; roll rate was high; a 360 deg turn could be completed within 24 seconds; stall recovery was good and the aircraft could be looped and Immelmanned at low airspeeds.

While in the air, the handling characteristics of the La-5 were exemplary, the fighter displayed some capriciousness during landing, tending to bounce alarmingly before settling down, and a number of aircraft were to be written off when their pilots applied power during bouncing, propeller torque turning them over. Also on the debit side were the lightweight nature of the La-5's armament and its inadequate range — the 105.5 Imp gal (480 l) five-tank arrangement had been inherited from the LaGG-3, but the adverse effect on manoeuvrability resulting from use of the two 14.3 Imp gal (65 l) outboard tanks led to these being filled only in overload condition for ferrying. Criticism of the range capability of the La-5 led to Lavochkin being summoned once again to the Kremlin. Several other designers, including Ilyushin, Myasishchev and Yakovlev, were present and Lavochkin's reception was very much more friendly than it had been on previous occasions. Stalin immediately demanded that the range of the La-5 be substantially increased. At this time, one of Lavochkin's deputies, L.A.Zaks, was working on the redesign of the fuel tank system, but Lavochkin was aware that this would have only a nominal effect on range owing to the critical CG problem. Lavochkin subsequently recalled the conversation as follows*:

"Stalin demanded that I increase the range of the fighter considerably. I replied, 'I cannot, *tovarishch* Stalin', and then explained the problem. Stalin then

*'The Life of Lavochkin' by Mikhail Arlazorov, Moscow 1969.

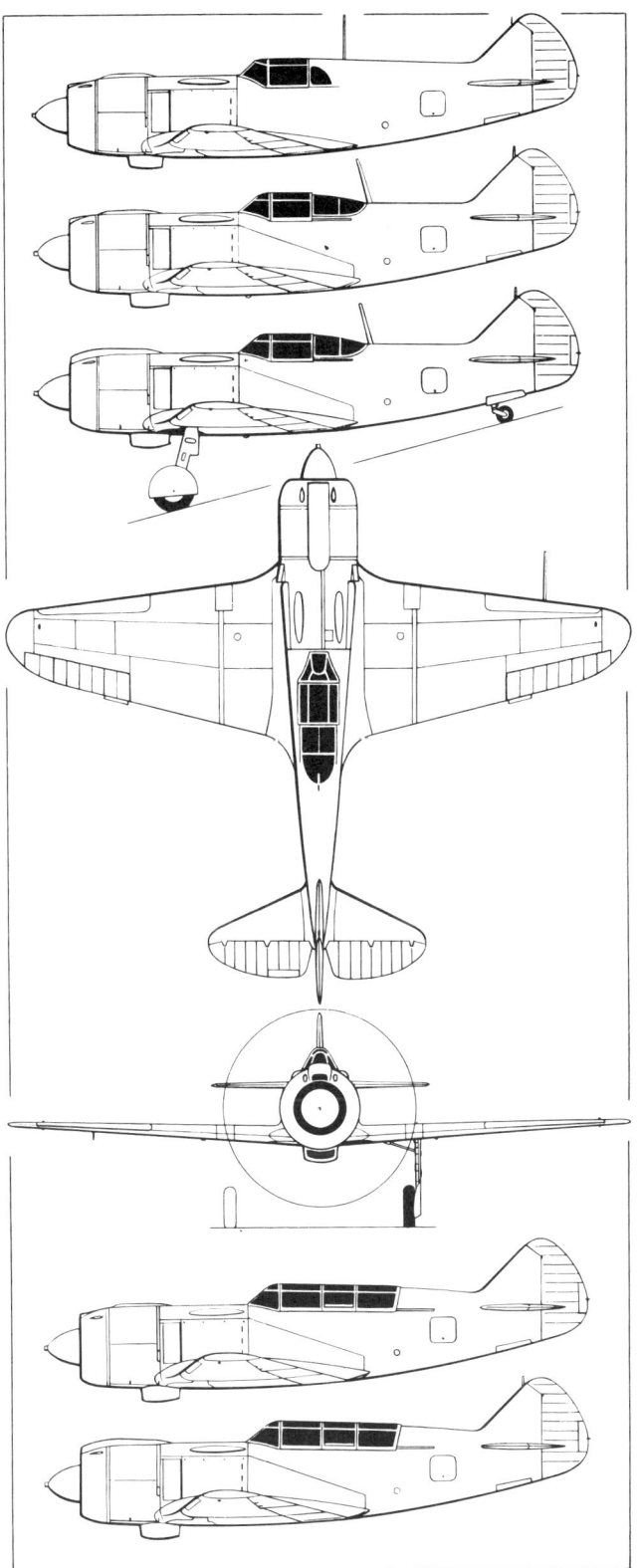

The side profiles at the head of the column above depict (top to bottom) the initial series La-5 (converted from LaGG-3 airframe), the initial production La-5 with the supercharger intake incorporated in the cowling ring and the La-5FN with the supercharger intake trunk extended forward above the ring. The La-5UTI profiles (immediately above) show the M-82F and M-82FN installations

The aesthetically appealing lines of the La-5FN are clearly illustrated by these photographs (above and foot of page) taken in April-May 1943. The close cowling of the Shvetsov M-82FN engine is particularly noteworthy

asked, 'So your aircraft cannot accommodate more fuel in any way?' I again answered in the negative, to which Stalin responded, 'Sit down and think about it for a while.' The other fighter designers present now all said that *they* could increase the range capabilities of *their* fighters and when it came to my turn to speak once more, I could do no more than reiterate the reasons why, in the case of my fighter, it was not possible. However, I added that I would like leave to consider the problem further and at this Stalin said jocularly to the meeting, 'Well, what can I do? He says he cannot do it; he obviously does'nt want to do it, but he'll think more on it! We'll have to leave it at that'."

Owing to the very close relationship to the LaGG-3, it was possible to introduce the La-5 on the assembly lines without any break in continuity of deliveries, and with the completion of the conversion of LaGG-3 airframes remaining in the factories, minor changes were introduced in new-production airframes, the principal of these being the cutting down of the aft fuselage decking and the introduction of a 360 deg-vision three-piece transparent canopy incorporating a 75-mm armourglass screen to protect the pilot's head and shoulders and an aft-sliding jettisonable section. An attempt was made to increase the damping capability of the shock absorbers, although this was to have little effect on the incipient bounce which characterised virtually every landing; an idiosyncrasy that was to remain with the La-5 throughout its production and service lives.

A further change introduced in the La-5 late in 1942 was the provision of the improved M-82F engine. Shvetsov's engine had been placed in production hurriedly and was still considered "immature" when making its service debut in the La-5. Cylinder head temperatures were critical — these had to be kept within the 200-220 deg C (392-428 deg F) range — and there were numerous instances of the cylinders *literally* losing their heads when the pilot failed to keep a wary

77 Imp gal (350 l) to 102 Imp gal (464 l). This change, together with other structural refinements, resulted in a saving of 353 lb (160 kg) in total airframe weight. Yet another change was made at the end of March 1943 when the M-82FN engine was phased in. The M-82FN (*Forsirovanny neprosredstvenno* — "Directly Boosted", but popularly and unofficially explained as indicating *Frontu nado*, or "Frontal need") differed from the preceding model of the engine in having direct fuel injection, this enabling a maximum output of 1,850 hp to be obtained at 2,500 rpm for take-off, but this power could be used for a maximum of two minutes only, output being otherwise similar to that of the carburettor-equipped M-82F. With this engine, the fighter was designated La-5FN and differed externally from earlier production models only in having the supercharger intake trunk fairing extended forward to the lip of the engine cowling.

By western standards, the La-5 was an unsophisticated aircraft and austerely equipped, but its sturdy wooden structure, its lack of complexity and the

While the handling qualities of the La-5FN once in the air were highly commended, the fighter excelling in close-in high-g manoeuvring style of combat, view for taxying and take-off was pronounced "deplorable" and the fighter suffered an incipient and dangerous bounce during landing

eye on the cylinder head temperature gauge. The loss of cylinder heads and even the complete disintegration of cylinders posed a serious problem for Arkadii Shvetsov's team during early service usage of the M-82, and an attempt to eradicate the difficulty combined with an increase in power was represented by the M-82F (*Forsirovanny* — "Boosted") which provided the same output as the initial model for take-off but gave 1,650 hp at 5,415 ft (1 650 m) and 1,450 hp at 15,255 ft (4 650 m) compared with 1,540 hp at 6,725 ft (2 050 m) and 1,330 hp at 17,715 ft (5 400 m). Aircraft fitted with the boosted engine were designated La-5F but did not differ externally from the new-production La-5s that had preceded them.

Some measure of the impetus placed behind the La-5 production programme may be gathered from the fact that, from the initiation of production in July 1942 to the end of that year, a total of 1,129 La-5s was delivered from the Gor'kiy and Tbilisi factories and production man hours per aircraft were reduced by 23 per cent (this was to be increased to 40 per cent over the next seven months). From early 1943, a further change was made on the assembly lines. The 14.3 Imp gal (65 l) fuel tanks in the outer wing panels — the use of which was restricted largely to ferry flights — were removed and, as a result of modification of the centre section, the three remaining tanks were increased in total capacity from

limited demands that it made on field maintenance in consequence rendered it manifestly suitable for the primitive conditions under which it was operated by the V-VS; conditions which would have resulted in a much lower rate of serviceability with a more sophisticated fighter. Its structure was virtually identical to that of the earlier LaGG-3, its fuselage being a semi-monocoque with plywood-sheathed birch frames, triangular-section wooden stringers and bakelite ply skinning, its three-section wing being built up on two *delta-drevesina* box spars and possessing the same bakelite ply covering, the tailplane having a similar structure to that of the wing and the tail fin being built integral with the fuselage. The movable control surfaces were metal-framed and fabric-covered, with the exception of the split flaps which were of plain dural sheet. Both the port elevator and rudder incorporated flight-adjustable Flettner-type tabs. Automatic leading-edge slats, hydraulically-operated wheel brakes and a steerable tailwheel were fitted. The mainwheels retracted inwards to lie side-by-side in the centre section, and the hydraulic system originally incorporated tailwheel retraction, but the retractable tailwheel proved troublesome in operation and was usually disconnected from the hydraulic system and locked in the extended position after delivery of the aircraft from the factory. Instrumentation was spartan;

(Left) MiG-3 flown by a zveno leader of a detached eskadril shot down over Karelian Isthmus in September 1942

(Immediately right) MiG-3 of the 401 IAP, August 1941. This IAP was commanded by V V Kokkinaki who had succeeded Lt Col Stepan P Suprun who had been killed in combat on 4 July 1941. (Below right) A LaGG-3 of an unidentified IAP flying in defence of Voronezh in the summer of 1942. The black-and-white propeller spinner indicated that this aircraft was flown by a zveno leader

(Below) LaGG-3 flown by Capt (later Col) Gerasim A Grigoryev, 6th Fighter Aviation Division, Moscow PVO, winter 1942-43. Note 15 'victory' stars on rear fuselage

(Below right) LaGG-3 brought down in combat with Finnish fighters over Karelia during the summer of 1942. Note the green-and-black upper surface camouflage

(Left) LaGG-3 operating over the Ukraine in the summer of 1942 during the German drive towards Voronezh. This particular aircraft employs the standard temperate zone camouflage scheme of the period with individual number on rudder

(Right) La-5FN presented to the V-VS by the Mongolian People's Republic. The emblem on the engine cowling indicates installation of the 'FN' version of the M-82 engine. (Below) La-7 flown by Ivan Kozhedub in the winter of 1944-45 with the 176 (formerly 19) 'Guards' IAP. The aircraft is that in which Kozhedub scored the last of his 62 'kills' (19 April 1945), at which time he was twice Hero of the Soviet Union (subsequently receiving the award for the third time)

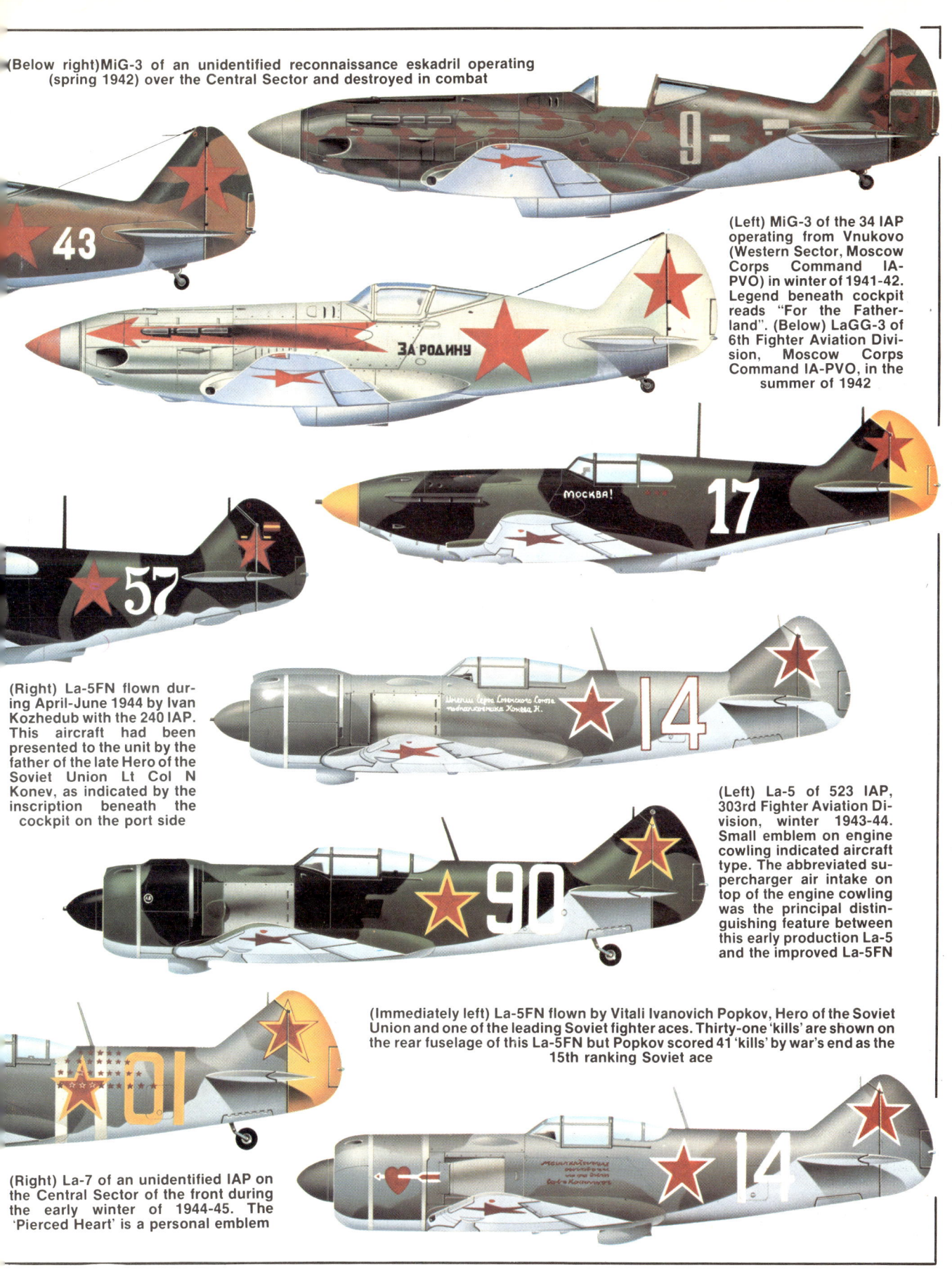

(Below right) MiG-3 of an unidentified reconnaissance eskadril operating (spring 1942) over the Central Sector and destroyed in combat

(Left) MiG-3 of the 34 IAP operating from Vnukovo (Western Sector, Moscow Corps Command IA-PVO) in winter of 1941-42. Legend beneath cockpit reads "For the Fatherland". (Below) LaGG-3 of 6th Fighter Aviation Division, Moscow Corps Command IA-PVO, in the summer of 1942

(Right) La-5FN flown during April-June 1944 by Ivan Kozhedub with the 240 IAP. This aircraft had been presented to the unit by the father of the late Hero of the Soviet Union Lt Col N Konev, as indicated by the inscription beneath the cockpit on the port side

(Left) La-5 of 523 IAP, 303rd Fighter Aviation Division, winter 1943-44. Small emblem on engine cowling indicated aircraft type. The abbreviated supercharger air intake on top of the engine cowling was the principal distinguishing feature between this early production La-5 and the improved La-5FN

(Immediately left) La-5FN flown by Vitali Ivanovich Popkov, Hero of the Soviet Union and one of the leading Soviet fighter aces. Thirty-one 'kills' are shown on the rear fuselage of this La-5FN but Popkov scored 41 'kills' by war's end as the 15th ranking Soviet ace

(Right) La-7 of an unidentified IAP on the Central Sector of the front during the early winter of 1944-45. The 'Pierced Heart' is a personal emblem

its PBP-1a gunsight was a rudimentary affair, reminiscent of early British reflector types, and its single-channel RSI-4 HF R/T set lacked reliability.

By the spring of 1943, the V-VS had begun to establish numerical air superiority over Germany's Eastern Front and the advent of the La-5 in quantity undoubtedly contributed to the rapid decline of the *Luftwaffe*. German fighter pilots reported that the La-5 in particular was being flown with considerably more elan and aggressiveness than had been generally displayed by Soviet fighters previously. This became particularly noticeable during the heavy commitment of the *Luftwaffe* in support of General Erich von Manstein's counter-offensive resulting, on 14 March, in the recapture of Kharkov*, and the subsequent *Zitadelle* offensive, while the fighting over the Orel-Kursk sector, where the La-5FN appeared in substantial numbers for the first time, resulted in the heaviest attrition suffered by the *Luftwaffe* over the Eastern Front to that time.

It was during the bitter Orel-Kursk fighting that a number of the top-scoring V-VS fighter pilots of WW II furthered or began to establish their reputations while flying the Lavochkin La-5, among them being Ivan N. Kozhedub who was to become the greatest ace of the V-VS. Kozhedub's regiment, the 240 IAP, had converted to the La-5 in February and had been held in reserve

---

**Von Manstein had miraculously halted the Soviet drive, despite odds of seven to one, and then, notwithstanding the weakened state of the Army Group 'B', counter-attacked successfully — one of the great military achievements of WW II.*

Apart from the V-VS, the La-5FN was flown operationally by the 1st Czechoslovak Fighter Regiment whose aircraft are seen at the head of this and the opposite page lined up on parade at Psheborsk airfield in Poland on 7 November 1944. The inscription on the cowling of the aircraft in the foreground above reads "Za slobodne Ceskoslovensko po boku Rude armady" ("For free Czechoslovakia by the side of the Red Army") Although unsuited for the fighter-bomber role, the La-5FN was frequently assigned this task and is seen (opposite page) with 55-lb (25-kg) underwing bombs at Zolna, near Zvolen, in September 1944. (Right) La-5FNs at the Tri duby (Three Oaks) base in October 1944, during operations in support of insurgents

(Above) La-5FN fighters of the 1st Czechoslovak Fighter Regiment at Proskurov, near Lvov in the Ukraine on 11 September 1944. (Left) A trio of La-5UTI tandem two-seaters during a ferry flight between Zitomir and Lvov, and (below) an La-5FN awaiting take-off instructions from Krosno airfield

until June, when it was assigned to the 16th Air Army. Flying an La-5 inscribed *Imeni Valeriya Chkalov*, Kozhedub gained his first "kill" on 6 July when he destroyed a Ju 87, and during the following autumn he was to claim 11 "kills" within 10 days over the Kiev region, ending the war with no fewer than 62 "kills" to become the top-scoring Soviet *and* Allied ace and one of only two fighter pilots to receive the title of Hero of the Soviet Union three times* . On the same day that Kozhedub claimed his first victory, another pilot flying the La-5 with the 171 IAP, A.K.Gorovets, saw, while returning alone from a mission, a large formation of Ju 87s. He succeeded in destroying nine of the enemy aircraft before he, in turn, was shot down and killed. Gorovets was awarded the title of Hero of the Soviet Union posthumously. The skies above the Orel-Kursk Front on 6 July also witnessed one of the most remarkable of the V-VS's fighter aces add to his score,

* *The other V-VS pilot to be designated Hero of the Soviet Union three times was Aleksandr I.Pokryshkin (see page 53) who successively flew the MiG-3, Bell P-39 Airacobra and La-7, and ended the war with 59 "kills" (48 of them claimed while flying the P-39 Airacobra).*

Aleksei P.Maras'ev. Maras'ev, who had claimed eight victories while flying Yak-1s, had had both legs amputated after being shot down in 1942, but had returned to his regiment, which had meanwhile re-equipped with the La-5, and flew his first combat mission on 6 July, shooting down a Ju 87 and claiming three Fw 190s on the following day, ending the war with a total of 19 "kills".

Many other V-VS fighter pilots attained 'ace' status while flying the La-5, such as Kirill A.Yevstigneyev of Kozhedub's regiment, who, during October 1943, claimed 12 victories in nine missions, becoming the joint fifth-ranking V-VS ace (with Arsenii V.Vorozheikin) with a total of 52 "kills", and Vitali I.Popkov who was to score a total of 41. In addition to Soviet fighter regiments, the La-5FN was flown by the two squadrons of the 1st Czechoslovak Fighter Regiment which was formed with a nucleus of highly experienced Czechoslovak pilots who had previously flown with the RAF. Converted to the La-5FN at Ivanovo and Kubinka in the spring of 1944, the Regiment was sent to the aid of Slovak insurgents on 17

(Right) Czechoslovak-flown La-5FNs photographed during a formation training flight from Ivanovo, northeast of Moscow, during training with the V-VS's No 6 Reserve Brigade, and (below) a Czechoslovak-flown La-5FN about to takeoff on an intercept mission from the Tri duby (Three Oaks) base

The La-5FN illustrated on this page was force-landed behind the German lines in 1943, restored to airworthy condition and flight tested by the Luftwaffe. The Luftwaffe considered the La-5FN to be a rather primitive war-plane and inadequately equipped, being particularly deficient in firepower. Instrmentation was pronounced unreliable, the gun sight ineffective and the hydraulic system troublesome.

September, operating from an airfield known as Tri Duby (Three Oaks), flying its first mission against the *Luftwaffe* base at Piestany on the following day. By the time the Czechoslovak-flown La-5FNs arrived at Tri Duby, the area over which the Slovak insurgents had gained control was shrinking rapidly under pressure from the *Wehrmacht* and on 25 October, the 11 surviving airworthy fighters of the 21 originally flown to Slovakia were ordered to return to Soviet-held territory, the Slovak National Uprising having proved abortive.

While changes introduced on the La-5 assembly lines were minimal during 1942-43 in order to adhere to the continually-repeated slogan "Do not touch the production line" so as to maximise deliveries to the V-VS, the idiosyncrasies displayed by the La-5 during landing had provided the principal motivation for the development of a tandem two-seat version intended primarily for conversion training but having a secondary high-speed liaison role. Designated La-5UTI (but sometimes referred to as the UTLa-5), the suffix indicating *Uchebnotrenirovochny istrebitel*, literally 'Instructional Training Fighter', the two-seater was initially produced by the conversion of La-5 and La-5F single-seaters on a special line established at a maintenance and overhaul factory, the first of these being assigned to regiments engaged in converting to the new Lavochkin fighter in October-November 1942. Subsequently, several La-5UTIs were assigned to each La-5-equipped regiment and in addition to providing 30-60 minutes dual instruction (usually including five-six take-offs and landings) for pilots newly assigned to the regiment, they were used for ferrying an advance guard of ground personnel when the regiment was transferred from one base to another, liaison duties and, on occasions, tactical reconnaissance. The La-5UTI was a straightforward adaptation of the single-seater in which a second cockpit was inserted aft of the radio bay, this being provided with duplicate control column and rudder pedals, and only the primary instruments. Both cockpits were enclosed by aft-sliding hoods, a fixed section enclosing the radio bay to provide a continuous "greenhouse" fairing into the normal aft fuselage decking; the tail surface control runs were re-routed; the tail fin was enlarged; the radio mast was moved from the fuselage spine and canted from the starboard side of the fuselage, and usually the starboard 20-mm ShVAK cannon was removed. During the summer of 1943, La-5UTI two-seaters with the M-82FN engine were interspersed on the La-5FN assembly lines.

The La-5FN was claimed to be particularly easily maintained under austere operating conditions. Engine accessibility was very good, the cowling incorporating four hinged sections as seen below. The cowling of the La-7 (see page 36) makes interesting comparison

An La-5FN photographed at Prague-Letnany in the summer of 1945. This type of fighter was largely relegated to the operational training role in the post-WW II Czechoslovak air arm and was also employed in small numbers by the paramilitary Air Police

The La-5 was largely confined to the low- and medium-altitude air superiority role, but was, on occasions, assigned the close support task, attacking enemy artillery positions, armour and transport for which it was anything but ideal owing to its relatively high vulnerability to groundfire. When employed on these missions it carried such underwing loads as four or six 82-mm RS-82 rocket projectiles, two 110-lb (50-kg) and two 55-lb (25-kg) bombs, or a pair of 220-lb (100-kg) bombs. The bombs were usually released in a 45 deg dive at an altitude of about 1,300 ft (400 m). If cloud forced the La-5 pilot to descend lower to drop his bombs, it was general practice to do so in a climb, turning steeply as the bombs were released.

In the autumn of 1943, with the La-5FN established in service, supplies of steel and light alloys became less critical and the *Narkomavprom* (State Commissariat of the Aviation Industry) deemed that some relaxation of the "Do not touch the production line" maxim was now permissible. Indeed, this was desirable if improved fighters were to be available to counter more advanced *Luftwaffe* fighters that it was anticipated would soon be deployed on the Eastern Front. The Lavochkin OKB therefore initiated the further development of the La-5 but now substituting metal wing spars for the wooden spars featured by all previous Lavochkin fighter models. Two main lines of development were pursued: one being the substitution of a wing of mixed construction for the wooden wing of the La-5FN and the other being the mating of this wing to an aerodynamically refined fuselage with the aim of extracting the maximum possible performance from the fundamental design without entailing the delay that would undoubtedly be incurred if a new and more powerful engine (such as the M-71) be introduced.

The new spar employed chromansil steel flanges and dural webs and its introduction resulted in a saving of 379 lb (172 kg) in structural weight and also permitted a useful increase in fuel tank capacity to 123 Imp gal (560 l). The new wing did not, in fact, appear on the La-5FN assembly lines until the late spring of 1944, by which time the Lavochkin fighter was also being manufactured by factories at Moscow and Yaroslavl. Almost simultaneously, the first production deliveries were to commence of the derivative of the basic design, which, utilising the same wing, embodied a number of aerodynamic refinements and had been assigned the designation La-7.

By the time that the La-5 was finally withdrawn from production late in 1944, a total of 9,920 fighters of this type had left the four factories that had been committed to its manufacture. Apart from the late production batches featuring metal spars, the La-5 had been the last first-line single-seat fighter of classic wooden construction to be employed by any of the combatants and in the day of mixed and all-metal construction this endowed Lavochkin's fighter with a weight penalty, a fact rendering all the more remarkable the performance of which it was capable. The Lavochkin team never succeeded in eradicating the La-5's penchant for emulating a kangaroo during landing — it was to be said that the Lavochkin that didn't bounce was a Focke-Wulf! In every other respect, however, it was a pilot's aeroplane and one for which its pilots developed an abiding affection. The combination of wing loading, power-to-weight ratio and aileron area — at 8.02 per cent of the total wing area this was proportionately the largest of any fighter of its period — resulted in a superlatively manoeuvrable warplane and the ideal dog-fighter. Perhaps surprisingly, in view of its wooden structure and ply skinning, it withstood climatic extremes well, yet few Soviet operational fields could offer the luxury of covered accommodation, and it was less demanding in terms of field maintenance than any of its contemporaries. Thus, by any standard, the La-5 may be considered as one of the outstanding combat aircraft of World War II.

La-5FN Specification

Power Plant: One Shvetsov M-82FN (ASh-82FN) 14-cylinder two-row radial air-cooled engine with two-stage supercharger and direct fuel injection rated at 1,850 hp at 2,500 rpm (for two minutes), 1,650 hp at 2,400 rpm at 5,415 ft (1 650 m) and 1,450 hp at 2,400 rpm at 15,255 ft (4 650 m), driving a VISh-105V three-bladed controllable-pitch metal propeller of 9.84-ft (3,00-m) diameter. Total fuel capacity of 102 Imp gal (464 l) distributed between three tanks in the wing centre section.
Performance: Max speed (at 7,100 lb/3 220 kg), 342 mph (550 km/h) at sea level, 348 mph (560 km/h) at 1,640 ft (500 m), 360 mph (580 km/h) at 4,920 ft (1 500 m), 370 mph (595 km/h) at 6,560 ft (2 000 m), 378 mph (608 km/h) at 11,480 ft (3 500 m), 386 mph (622 km/h) at 16,405 ft (5 000 m), 403 mph (648 km/h) at 20,670 ft (6 300 m), 382 mph (615 km/h) at 22,965 ft (7 000 m); time to 16,405 ft (5 000 m), 4.7 min; service ceiling, 31,170 ft (9 500 m); endurance at max continuous power, 35 min, at best econ power (1 600 rpm), 1 hr 10 min; max range at econ cruise, 475 mls (765 km).
Weights: Empty equipped, 6,173 lb (2 800 kg); normal loaded, 7,407 lb (3 360 kg).
Dimensions: Span, 32 ft $1^{4}/_{5}$ in (9,80 m); length, 28 ft $2^{3}/_{5}$ in (8,60 m); height, 8 ft 4 in (2,54 m); wing area, 188.37 sq ft (17,50 m^2).
Armament: Two 20-mm Shpital'ny-Vladimirov (ShVAK) cannon synchronised to fire through the propeller disc with 200 rpg and provision for four or six 82-mm RS-82 rockets, two 110-lb (50-kg) and two 55-lb (25-kg) bombs, or two 220-lb (100-kg) bombs.

The La-5FN presented an inexperienced pilot with severe problems during landing and training attrition was high, the aircraft illustrated right having suffered a heavy landing after the pilot had applied power during a "bounce". The La-5UTI remained in Czechoslovak service postwar and is seen below serving in 1945-46

LAVOCHKIN LA-7

Despite assignment of a new designation, the La-7, which began to reach operational V-VS fighter regiments in the late spring of 1944, was anything but a new design; it was rather the ultimate refinement of the basic La-5, embodying all the progressive changes incorporated in the earlier model during its production life and featuring various minor aerodynamic refinements which produced a moderate performance gain without any time-consuming redesign of fundamental components. The La-7 was essentially an interim measure, which, while carrying development of Semyon Lavochkin's first generation of fighters to its zenith, was intended to provide the V-VS with an improved performance pending the availability of an entirely new all-metal fighter synthesising the operational experience gained with Lavochkin's earlier progeny.

Development of the La-7 was initiated in the autumn of 1943 under the design bureau designation La-120* or *Samolet* 120, this incorporating the results of a TsAGI wind tunnel programme aimed at defining areas in which the basic La-5FN could be aerodynamically improved. Work on the La-120 was launched simultaneously with development of a modified wing structure in which the wooden box spars were to give place to new metal spars employing chromansil steel flanges and dural webs, the joint ribs between the centre section and outer panels being of dural but wood being retained for all other ribs, together with plywood skinning. This wing was intended for application both to the standard La-5FN and to the aerodynamically refined fighter.

Closest attention was paid to the refinement of the cowling for the M-82FN engine. The long supercharger air intake fairing was removed from the upper centreline of the cowling and replaced by a flush intake in the port wing root and the oil cooler intake was transferred from the bottom of the cowling to a position under the fuselage level with the wing trailing edge. The cowling itself — which, on the La-5FN, comprised four hinged and two fixed sections — comprised only two segments aft of the front ring, these hingeing upwards on the top centreline to facilitate maintenance. The starter dog was removed from the spinner of the 10.17-ft (3,10-m) diameter VISh-105V-4 propeller, tailwheel retraction was restored and hinged flaps were attached to the fuselage centreline to enclose the previously-exposed portions of the mainwheels when retracted. Continuous taper was applied to the wing centre-section leading edge — the sharply-tapered root leading edges of the La-5FN being eliminated — and in addition to the supercharger intake, gun cooling apertures were introduced in the wing roots. Apart from the relocation of some items of equipment and marginally less spartan instrumentation, the revised fighter was in other respects essentially similar to the La-5FN.

The prototype La-120 was flown for the first time in November 1943 by N.V.Adamovich and immediately demonstrated a worthwhile improvement in performance. During the test programme conducted in the winter of 1943-44, the La-120 recorded a maximum speed of 422 mph (680 km/h) at 9,840 ft (3 000 m) and proved capable of attaining an altitude of 16,405 ft (5 000 m) in 4.45 minutes. In the spring of 1944, it was ordered into production as the La-7 at factories in Moscow and Yaroslavl, the intended armament being three 20-mm Berezina B-20 lightweight cannon

The considerable improvement in engine accessibility achieved with the La-7 by comparison with the earlier La-5 may be assessed if these photographs are compared with that of the La-5 on page 33

---

*A system of design bureau designations had been instituted by the Lavochkin OKB with the La-5 which was referred to as the La-110, the second digit being changed for each new type (ie, La-120 for the La-7, La-130 for the La-9, La-140 for the La-11, etc), the third digit being changed to indicate a significant modification of the basic design (ie, La-121, La-122, etc).

The La-7 above, photographed during the winter of 1944-45, belonged to an unidentified Guards IAP and was unusual among V-VS fighters in having a personal emblem (a heart pierced by an arrow) on the engine cowling

mounted asymmetrically in the forward fuselage, two to port and one to starboard. These weapons, each weighing only 55 lb (25 kg) as compared with the 92.6 lb (42 kg) of the ShVAK, possessed the same rate of fire and muzzle velocity as the heavier weapon, thus providing a heavier weight of fire at an appreciably lower installed weight. In the event, shortfalls in the supply of B-20s led to the three-gun installation being applied only to those La-7s built at the Yaroslavl factory, these being unofficially known as "Yaroslavl La-7s", while those built in Moscow reverted to the twin-ShVAK installation of the La-5FN. It was generally believed that the "Yaroslavl La-7s" were of a higher manufacturing standard than were the "Moskva La-7s" — certainly one batch of Moscow-built La-7s had to undergo modifications as a result of a series of spar attachment

The cleaner lines of the La-7 by comparison with the La-5 and resulting from the removal of the supercharger and oil cooler intakes from the engine cowling are apparent in this view of an early production example

During the final weeks of WW II, the La-7 began to be issued to the 1st Czechoslovak Fighter Regiment as a replacement for the unit's La-5FNs and an example of this fighter in Czechoslovak service is seen left at the Balice airfield, near Krakow in Poland, in April 1945. The La-7 was destined to remain the principal Czechoslovak single-seat fighter for several postwar years and was generally popular with its pilots

Lavochkin La-7 Cutaway Key

1 Propeller spinner
2 VISh-105V-4 three-blade controllable-pitch metal propeller
3 Controllable frontal intake louvres
4 Semi-circular upward-hinging engine access panels (port and starboard)
5 ShVAK cannon port
6 Shvetsov M-82FN 14-cylinder radial air-cooled engine
7 Exhaust pipe cluster (seven per side)
8 Cooling air exit louvre (port and starboard)
9 Tubular steel engine bearer
10 Port belt-fed gas-operated 20-mm ShVAK cannon (standard for 'Moskva La-7')
11 Port cannon ammunition tank (200 rounds)
12 Starboard cannon breech fairing
13 Oil tank
14 Laminated wooden block bulkhead reinforcement
15 Cockpit bulkhead
16 Armourglass (60-mm) windscreen
17 PBP-1a reflector sight
18 Pitot head
19 Starboard navigation light
20 Aft-sliding cockpit canopy
21 Instrument display panels
22 Control column
23 Engine throttle control
24 Engine air louvre controls
25 Oxygen regulator
26 Oil cooler control
27 Pilot's seat (parachute pan)
28 Armour plate (8-mm)
29 Armourglass screen (75-mm)
30 Radio packs (RSI-6)
31 Oxygen bottle
32 Rear spar/fuselage attachment
33 Port inter-spar fuel tank (matching centre and starboard tanks)
34 Mainspar/fuselage attachment
35 Mainwheel well
36 Mainwheel well doors
37 Hydraulic retraction jack
38 Undercarriage retraction pivot
39 Gun-cooling air intake (port and starboard)

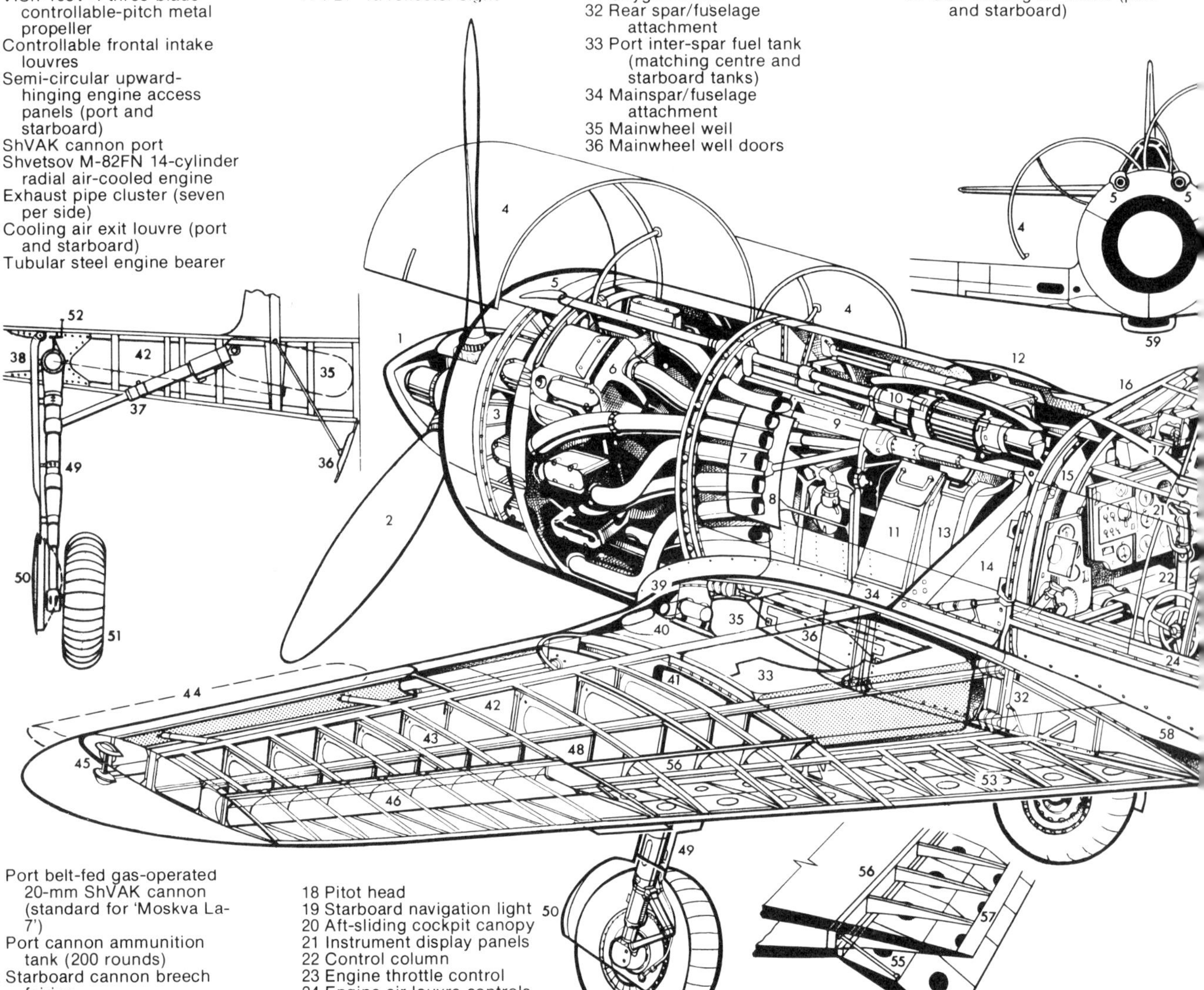

point failures that occurred on these aircraft while being dived.

Production La-7s began to reach the frontline V-VS regiments in the late spring and early summer of 1944, among the first to re-equip being the 176 (formerly 19) Guards (Proskurovsky Order of the Red Banner and of Aleksandr Nevsky) IAP to which Ivan N.Kozhedub — at that time the second-ranking V-VS ace with 45 confirmed victories — was transferred on 19 August 1944, when the IAP was based at Brest-Litovsk as part of General Rudenko's 16th Air Army. By the end of the year, Kozhedub had made a further 12 "kills" while flying the La-7, and on 15 February 1945, he succeeded in shooting down an Me 262 jet fighter, the first to be seen over the front. The regiment commanded by the V-VS's then top-scoring ace, Aleksandr I.Pokryshkin (eventually pushed into second place by Kozhedub), also converted to the La-7 at this time, exchanging its P-39N Airacrobras for the Lavochkins in August 1944.

Several variants of the basic La-7 were under development during the summer of 1944. A tandem two-seat model, the La-7UTI, for conversion training and high-speed liaison tasks, was built in parallel with the standard single-seater, this having a similar tandem seating arrangement to that of the La-5UTI with armament restricted to a single ShVAK cannon in the portside upper decking. On some examples the oil cooler intake fairing was restored to the position that it occupied on the La-5FN and La-5UTI.

Another variant was the rocket-boosted La-7R (*Raketny* or "Rocket") on which work was initiated in the early summer of 1944 as a potential counter to the threat of a high-altitude bombing offensive against Moscow by the *Luftwaffe*. Two prototypes of the La-7R were produced by the conversion of standard production aircraft to take an RD-1KhZ auxiliary rocket motor

40 Supercharger air intake (matching starboard auxiliary intake)
41 Dural rib structure mating outer panel and centre section
42 Forward wing spar (chromansil steel flanges and dural webs)
43 Wooden ribs
44 Automatic leading edge slat (obliquely-operated)
45 Port navigation light
46 Dural-framed fabric-covered aileron
47 Aileron hinge datum line (showing underside leading edge balancing)
48 Rear wing spar (chromansil steel flanges and dural webs)
49 Oleo-pneumatic mainwheel strut
50 Mainwheel cover plate
51 Mainwheel (650 x 200 mm)
52 Pilot's visual undercarriage position indicator
53 Port wing flap (plain dural sheet structure)
54 Flap shown lowered 30 deg
55 Flap actuating rod
56 Auxiliary spar (carrying control surfaces)
57 Fixed trailing edge
58 Wing root fairing
59 Oil cooler air intake
60 Oil cooler
61 Variable air outlet
62 Compressed air filler cap
63 Compressed air bottles
64 Aerial mast
65 Bakelite-ply skinning
66 Semi-monocoque fuselage construction
67 Accumulator access panel
68 Accumulator
69 Rudder cables
70 Lift point
71 Wooden two-spar tailplane (plywood skin)
72 Metal-framed fabric-covered elevator
73 Elevator trim tab
74 Tailplane/fuselage attachments
75 Wooden fin structure (integral with fuselage)
76 Aerial attachment stub
77 Rudder hinge post
78 Metal-framed fabric-covered rudder
79 Rudder trim tab
80 Tail navigation light
81 Rudder hinge (lowest of three)
82 Aft-retracting tailwheel (300 x 125 mm)
83 Tailwheel doors
84 Oleo-pneumatic tailwheel leg pivot
85 Tailwheel retraction jack
86 Elevator control linkage rods

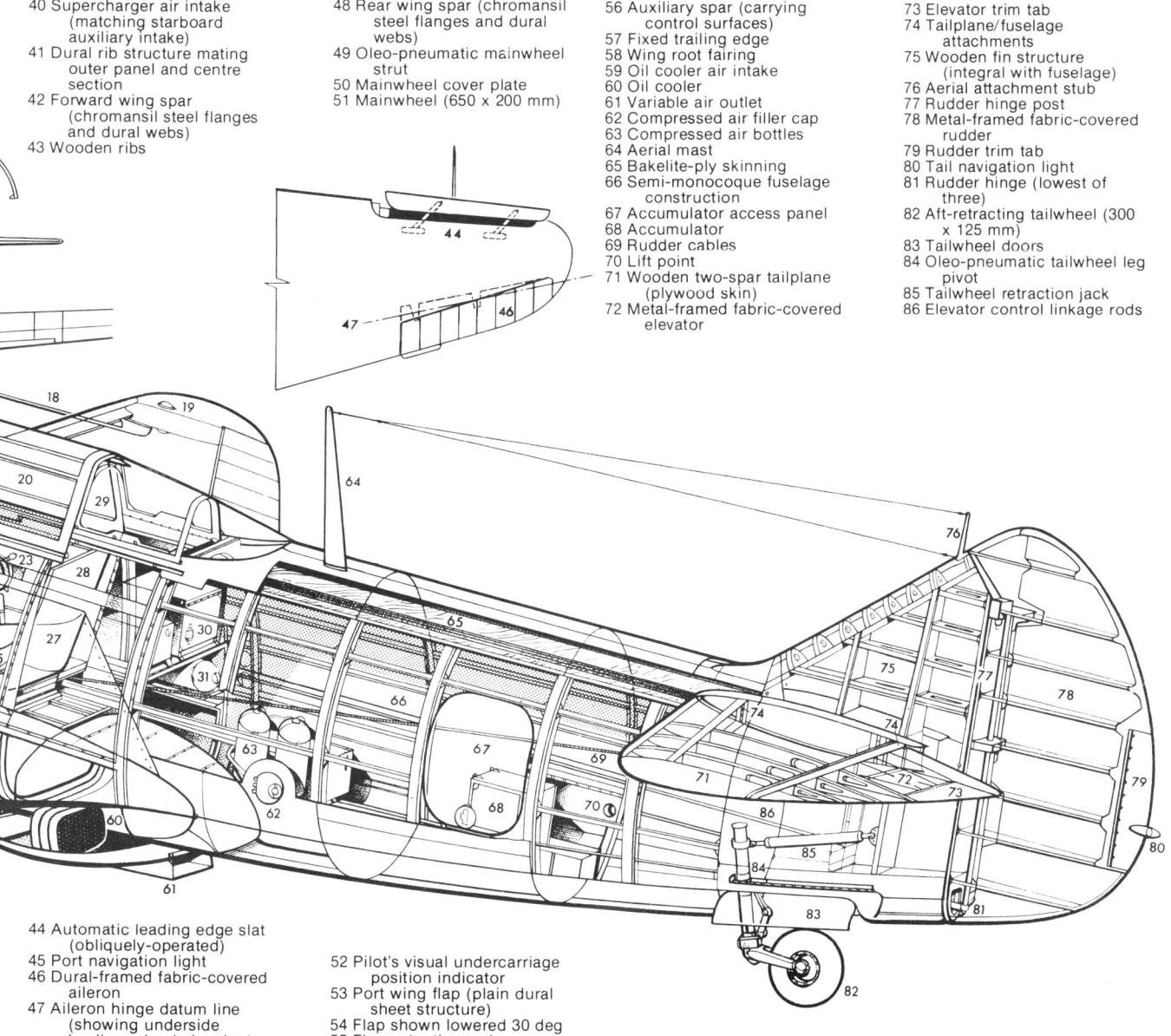

(Left) An La-7 on display in the Frunze Central House of Aviation in Moscow and allegedly that flown by Ivan N.Kozhedub but incorrectly sporting three "Hero of the Soviet Union" decorations whereas the third was not awarded until Kozhedub had ceased flying. (Below left) An La-7UTI landed by a V-VS defector in Turkey. It will be noted that this aircraft, unlike that illustrated at the foot of the page, has its oil cooler repositioned beneath the engine cowling

in the extreme tail. Developed by S.P.Korolev and V.P.Glushko, the RD-1KhZ operated on nitric acid and kerosene and provided 660 lb (300 kg) thrust for three minutes. The fuel tanks for the rocket motor were installed aft of the radio bay and the base of the rudder was cut away to allow for the extension of the rear fuselage to accommodate the auxiliary power plant itself. After protracted ground trials, an initial flight test was attempted in October 1944 by Georgi M.Shiyanov. During the take-off run, however, a fuel pipe failed and the rocket motor exploded, the aircraft catching fire and Shiyanov "baling out".

Shiyanov continued the flight test programme with the second prototype La-7R, but on one occasion, when relighting the rocket motor in flight, there was an explosion which left virtually no elevator surface and only 25 per cent of the rudder. Nevertheless, by skilful piloting, Shiyanov succeeded in landing safely, and, after repairs had been effected managed to attain speeds in excess of 435 mph (700 km/h) in level flight. Flight testing of the La-7R was to continue until February

1945 under low priority, the threat to Moscow of high-altitude bombing having meanwhile been removed, but was abandoned when the plywood skinning began to disintegrate as a result of the corrosive effect of the nitric acid vapour escaping from the inadequately-sealed tank. A further rocket-boosted example — a conversion of one of the original prototype airframes and therefore referred to as the La-120R — had been completed by this time and, flown initially in January 1945 by A.V.Davidov, this had an improved version of the RD-1KhZ rocket motor (referred to as the ZhRD-1) and a revised installation, the local airframe structure having been changed from wood to metal. With the same thrust and endurance as the rocket in the La-7R, the ZhRD-1 boosted the maximum level speed of the La-120R by 45 mph (72 km/h) to 461 mph (742 km/h) at 9,840 ft (3 000 m). The test programme with the La-120R was to be continued after WW II, the aircraft being demonstrated publicly over Tushino in August 1946.

In parallel with the La-7R programme, the Lavochkin OKB endeavoured to improve the high-altitude intercept capabilities of the La-7 by turbo-supercharging its M-82FN engine. Designated La-7TK and test flown during July-August 1944, this experimental version was fitted with a pair of TsIAM-developed TK-3 turbo-superchargers and achieved a maximum speed of 420 mph (676 km/h) during testing which terminated abruptly when one of the turbo-superchargers exploded and the aircraft was destroyed. Simultaneously, testing was undertaken with an La-7 fitted with a turbo-supercharged ASh-71TK engine of 2,000 hp, but the erratic behaviour of the TsIAM turbo-superchargers was compunded by the poor reliability of the Shvetsov engine and trials were soon discontinued. Yet a further experimental La-7 was fitted with the 2,000 hp ASh-83 radial. Mounting a pair of 23-mm Nudelman-Suranov NS-23 cannon, this variant was flown in February 1945 and achieved 450 mph (725 km/h) at 24,280 ft (7 400 m) during its flight test programme, but development was abandoned with the decision not to place the ASh-83 engine in production.

By the end of 1944, the Lavochkin OKB had abandoned the further development of the mixed-construction La-7 in favour of an entirely new all-metal design bearing only a configurational similarity to its predecessors. Several all-metal developments of the La-7 were projected and discarded before work began, early in 1945, on the La-126, which, despite its design bureau designation which suggested that it was a further development of the La-120, possessed no commonality apart from an ASh-82FN engine with any preceding fighter. The La-126 (which, as the La-126PVRD, was to be used to test Bondaryuk VRD-430 ramjets in the summer of 1946) featured an all-metal monocoque fuselage and laminar-flow wings, but did not commence its flight test programme until after the end of WW II. With minor changes, the La-126 served as the basis for the La-130 which was to enter production for the V-VS as the La-9.

The La-7 was a dog-fighter supreme, emulating its immediate predecessor in that it excelled in close-in

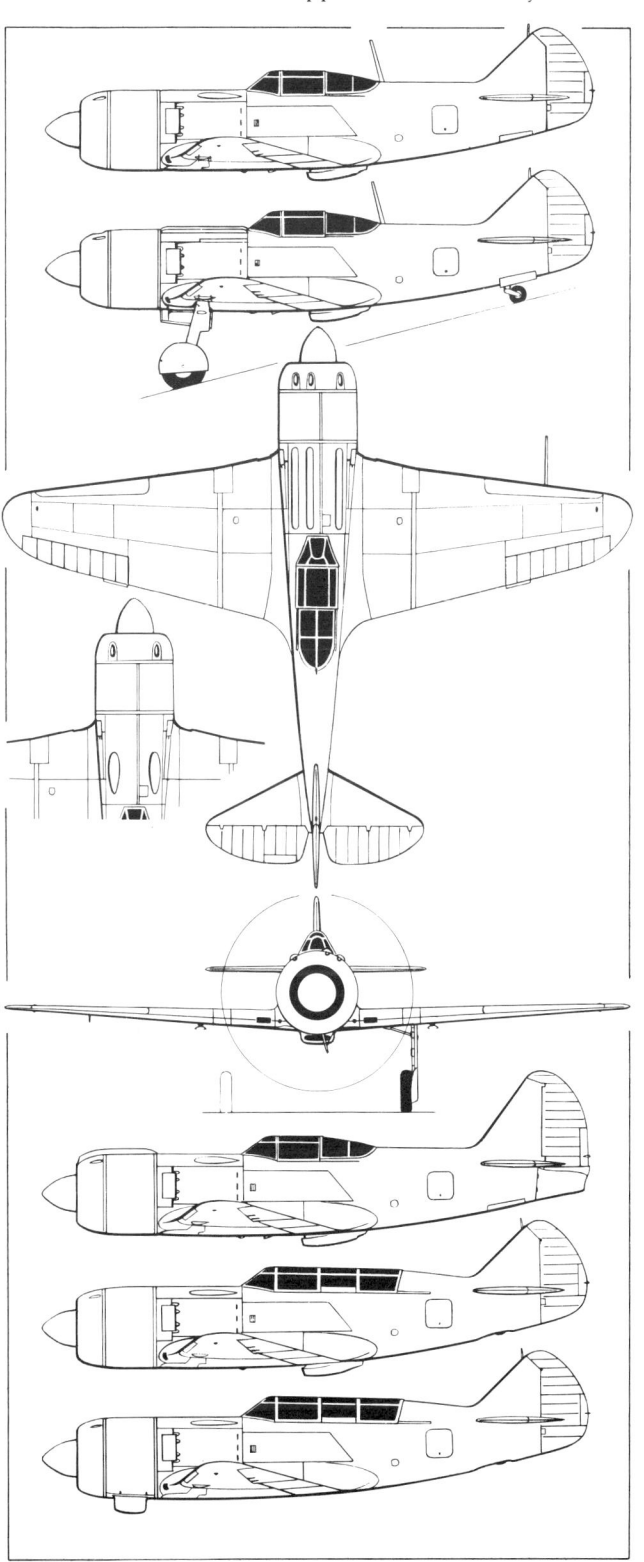

The side profiles immediately below depict (top) the "Moskva La-7" and the "Yaroslavl La-7", the plan and head-on views relating to the latter and the inset scrap view to the former. The side profiles at the foot of the column depict (top) the experimental rocket-boosted La-7R and (below) the two versions of the La-7UTI, the bottom view illustrating the relocated oil cooler applied to some aircraft

high-g manoeuvring combat, particularly at low altitudes where its aileron turns were allegedly unbeatable. Its handling characteristics were essentially similar to those of the La-5FN, but were referred to by its pilots as "indefinably better", and the tendency to bounce on landing, which was so much a part of the character of the earlier fighter, while not eradicated, was notably less vicious. The La-7 assumed progressively greater importance during the last nine months of the conflict in Europe and played a major role in the fighting over Germany in the last months of the war. Although it made provision for two 220-lb (100-kg) bombs underwing, it was employed almost exclusively in the air superiority role, the "Yaroslavl La-7" proving particularly efficacious in that it offered a weight of fire of 8.46 lb/sec (3,84 kg/sec) as compared with the 5.64 lb/sec (2,56 kg/sec) of the "Moskva La-7". Apart from the 1st Czechoslovak Fighter Regiment, which began to receive the newer fighter as a replacement for its La-5FNs during the final weeks of WW II in Europe, the La-7 was employed exclusively by the V-VS and was to be finally withdrawn from first-line service late in 1947, production having terminated in 1946 with a total of 5,753 examples built. The La-7 soldiered on somewhat longer with the *Ceskoslovenske letectvo* from which it was finally withdrawn in 1950.

La-7 Specification
Power Plant: One Shvetsov M-82FN (ASh-82FN) 14-cylinder two-row radial air-cooled engine with two-stage supercharger and direct fuel injection rated at 1,850 hp at 2,500 rpm (for two minutes), 1,650 hp at 2,400 rpm at 5,415 ft (1 650 m) and 1,450 hp at 2,400 rpm at 15,255 ft (4 650 m), driving a VISh-105V-4 three-bladed controllable-pitch metal propeller of 10.17 ft (3,10-m) diameter. Total fuel capacity of 134 Imp gal (610 l) distributed between three tanks in the wing centre section.
Performance: Max speed (at 7,010 lb/3 180 kg), 371 mph (597 km/h) at sea level, 379 mph (610 km/h) at 3,280 ft (1 000 m), 399 mph (643 km/h) at 6,560 ft (2 000 m), 416 mph (670 km/h) at 9,845 ft (3 000 m), 410 mph (660 km/h) at 13,125 ft (4 000 m), 423 mph (680 km/h) at 19,030 ft (5 800 m), 416 mph (670 km/h) at 21,325 ft (6 500 m); time to 16,405 ft (5 000 m), 4.52 min; service ceiling, 31,170 ft (9 500 m); range at econ cruise, 616 mls (990 km).
Weights: Empty equipped, 5,842 lb (2 650 kg); normal loaded, 7,496 lb (3 400 kg).
Dimensions: Span, 32 ft 11$^{4/5}$ in (9,80 m); length, 28 ft 2$^{3/5}$ in (8,60 m); height, 8 ft 6¼ in (2,60 m); wing area, 189.34 sq ft (17,59 m^2).
Armament: Two 20-mm Shpital'ny-Vladimirov (ShVAK) cannon with 200 rpg or three 20-mm Berezina B-20 cannon with 170 rpg synchronised to fire through the propeller disc. Provision for two 220-lb (100-kg) bombs or six 82-mm RS-82 rockets on underwing racks.

The La-7R (above and below) was a rocket-boosted version evolved as a potential countermeasure for a threatened bombing offensive against Moscow in 1944. Two prototypes of the La-7R were produced, the first of these being illustrated

MIKOYAN-GUREVICH MIG-3

In the late spring of 1941, a German delegation led by the air attache in Moscow, *Oberst* (later *Generalleutnant*) Heinrich Aschenbrenner, visited *Zavod* 1, the largest of two aircraft factories at Khodinka, Moscow's Central Airport, where it was shown the assembly lines of a new fighter monoplane, which, the delegation's Soviet hosts announced, was the MiG-3 and "already in service in large numbers with our fighter aviation!" The same fighter was seen in substantial numbers at two airfields on the Moscow periphery to which the Germans were taken and while not so naive as to believe what it saw to be fully representative of V-VS equipment and afforded no means of assessing the MiG-3 as a combat aircraft, the German delegation was duly impressed.

The Soviet invitation had come as something of a surprise to the Germans when received in April 1941, and particularly so in view of the fact that, only a few weeks earlier, a Junkers Ju 86P of the 4. *Staffel* of the German High Command's reconnaissance wing, the *Aufklärungsgruppe Ob.d.L.*, had been forced down in inclement weather near Vinnitsa while performing a clandestine reconnaissance mission over Soviet territory and its *Luftwaffe* crew captured. The tension between Germany and the Soviet Union had never been higher and while Soviet motives behind the gesture were not immediately obvious, the invitation had been accepted with alacrity.

Soviet reasoning soon became abundantly clear. In a move reminiscent of the game of bluff and counterbluff played by France and Germany during the last year of

(Head of page) The first prototype of the MiG-1 which effected its initial flight at Khodinka on 5 April 1940, and (right) the MiG-1 in production form with open cockpit. The sideways-hinging canopy of the prototype and preproduction MiG-1s was deleted from production examples owing to the dislike of the V-VS service pilot of the restrictions on vision that the poor quality of the plexiglass imposed

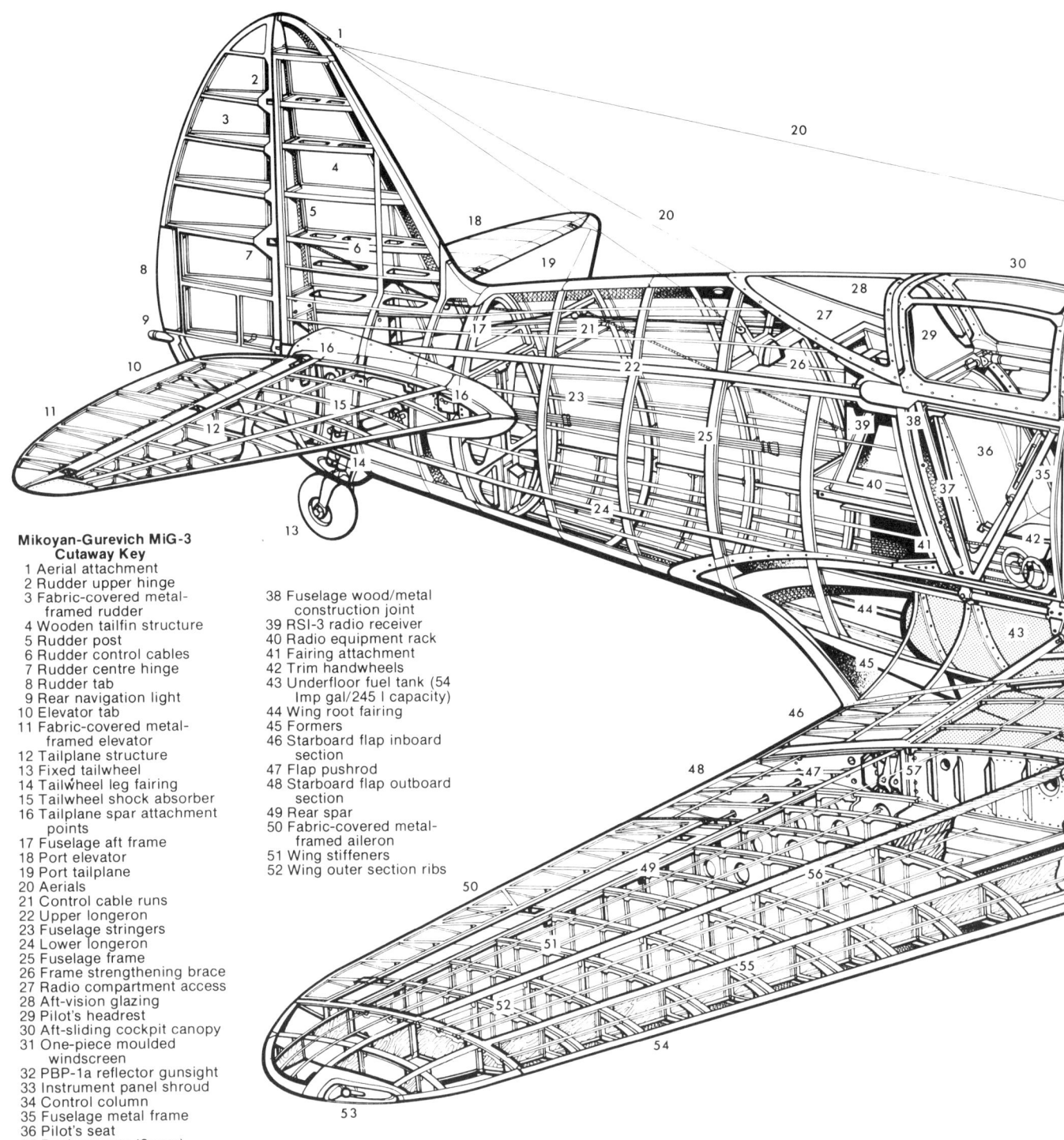

Mikoyan-Gurevich MiG-3 Cutaway Key
1 Aerial attachment
2 Rudder upper hinge
3 Fabric-covered metal-framed rudder
4 Wooden tailfin structure
5 Rudder post
6 Rudder control cables
7 Rudder centre hinge
8 Rudder tab
9 Rear navigation light
10 Elevator tab
11 Fabric-covered metal-framed elevator
12 Tailplane structure
13 Fixed tailwheel
14 Tailwheel leg fairing
15 Tailwheel shock absorber
16 Tailplane spar attachment points
17 Fuselage aft frame
18 Port elevator
19 Port tailplane
20 Aerials
21 Control cable runs
22 Upper longeron
23 Fuselage stringers
24 Lower longeron
25 Fuselage frame
26 Frame strengthening brace
27 Radio compartment access
28 Aft-vision glazing
29 Pilot's headrest
30 Aft-sliding cockpit canopy
31 One-piece moulded windscreen
32 PBP-1a reflector gunsight
33 Instrument panel shroud
34 Control column
35 Fuselage metal frame
36 Pilot's seat
37 Back armour (9-mm)
38 Fuselage wood/metal construction joint
39 RSI-3 radio receiver
40 Radio equipment rack
41 Fairing attachment
42 Trim handwheels
43 Underfloor fuel tank (54 Imp gal/245 l capacity)
44 Wing root fairing
45 Formers
46 Starboard flap inboard section
47 Flap pushrod
48 Starboard flap outboard section
49 Rear spar
50 Fabric-covered metal-framed aileron
51 Wing stiffeners
52 Wing outer section ribs

peace in Europe, in which delegations were exchanged and the respective hosts endeavoured to convince their guests that their respective re-equipment programmes had attained more advanced stages than had, in fact, been achieved, the Soviet government was anxious to create the impression that the defensive capabilities of its forces were greater than its intelligence reports informed it that Germany believed them to be. The Soviet motive was summed up succinctly during the delegation's visit to *Zavod* 1 by Artem I.Mikoyan, chief engineer of the factory and, as the Germans were informed, brother of Anastasias I.Mikoyan, the People's Commissar for Economics and Deputy Prime Minister. Mikoyan gave the delegation an unequivocal warning which none doubted to have been issued on the orders of the highest Soviet authority and which was to be quoted verbatim in Aschenbrenner's subsequent report to the *Generalstab der Luftwaffe*: "We have now

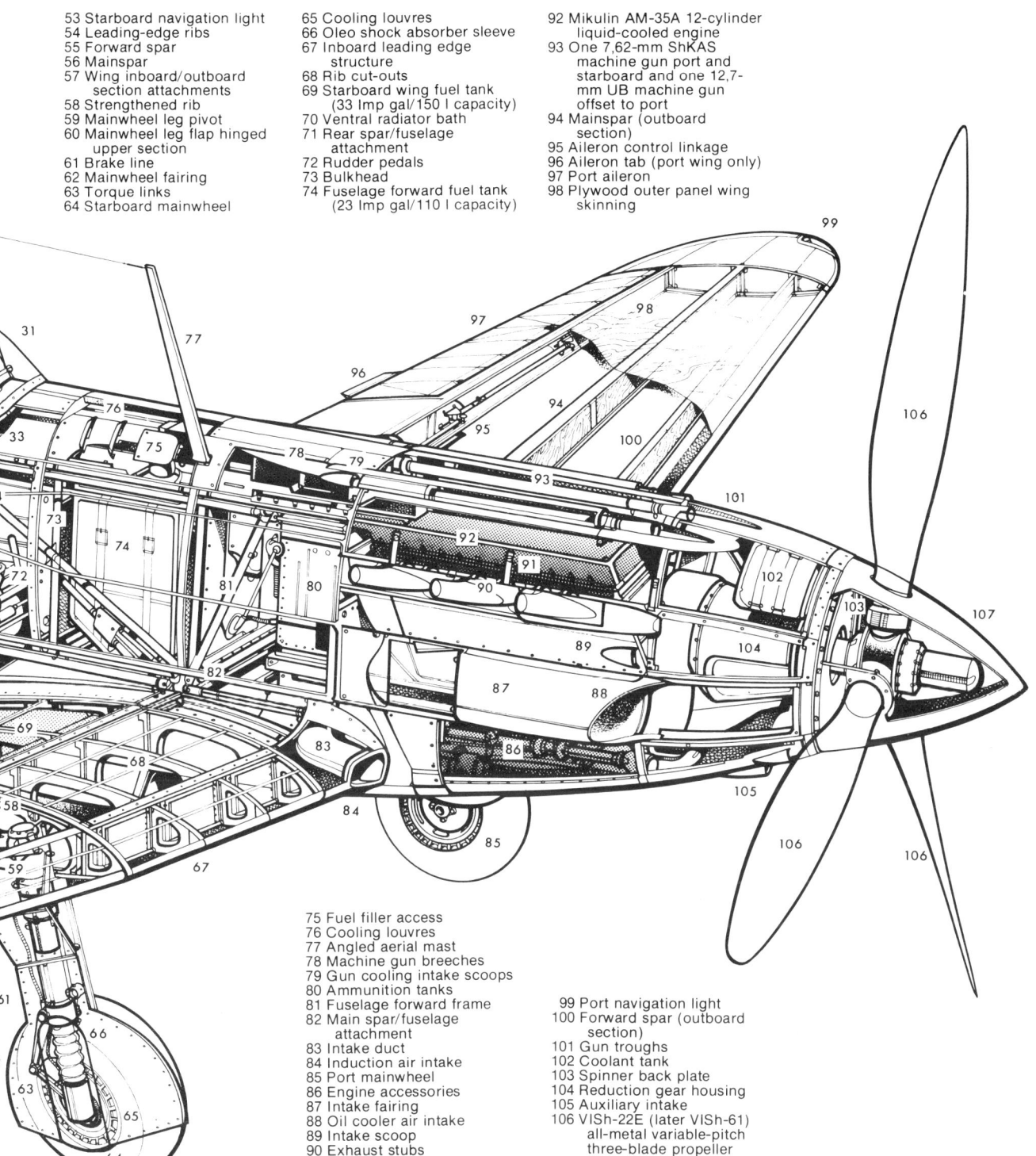

53 Starboard navigation light
54 Leading-edge ribs
55 Forward spar
56 Mainspar
57 Wing inboard/outboard section attachments
58 Strengthened rib
59 Mainwheel leg pivot
60 Mainwheel leg flap hinged upper section
61 Brake line
62 Mainwheel fairing
63 Torque links
64 Starboard mainwheel
65 Cooling louvres
66 Oleo shock absorber sleeve
67 Inboard leading edge structure
68 Rib cut-outs
69 Starboard wing fuel tank (33 Imp gal/150 l capacity)
70 Ventral radiator bath
71 Rear spar/fuselage attachment
72 Rudder pedals
73 Bulkhead
74 Fuselage forward fuel tank (23 Imp gal/110 l capacity)
75 Fuel filler access
76 Cooling louvres
77 Angled aerial mast
78 Machine gun breeches
79 Gun cooling intake scoops
80 Ammunition tanks
81 Fuselage forward frame
82 Main spar/fuselage attachment
83 Intake duct
84 Induction air intake
85 Port mainwheel
86 Engine accessories
87 Intake fairing
88 Oil cooler air intake
89 Intake scoop
90 Exhaust stubs
91 Cowling release catches
92 Mikulin AM-35A 12-cylinder liquid-cooled engine
93 One 7,62-mm ShKAS machine gun port and starboard and one 12,7-mm UB machine gun offset to port
94 Mainspar (outboard section)
95 Aileron control linkage
96 Aileron tab (port wing only)
97 Port aileron
98 Plywood outer panel wing skinning
99 Port navigation light
100 Forward spar (outboard section)
101 Gun troughs
102 Coolant tank
103 Spinner back plate
104 Reduction gear housing
105 Auxiliary intake
106 VISh-22E (later VISh-61) all-metal variable-pitch three-blade propeller
107 Spinner

shown you everything that we have and what we can do, and whoever attacks us we will destroy!"

Aschenbrenner's report to the *Generalstab* stressed the remarkable transformation in quality standards that appeared to have taken place in the Soviet aircraft industry and the fact that there could be no doubt that the performance of the MiG-3 was markedly in advance of the performances of Soviet fighters with which 5 *Abteilung*, the intelligence branch of the *Luftwaffe*, was familiar. Adolf Hitler's reaction to the report was to comment: "Well, you can see how far they have already progressed. We must begin [our attack] immediately!"

There were cogent reasons for having selected the MiG-3 assembly line to show the German delegation. The plans that had been drawn up in 1939 by the Defence Committee of the Council of People's Commissars (*Omitet oborony pri Sovete Narodnykh Kommisarov*) for the reconstruction and modernisation of

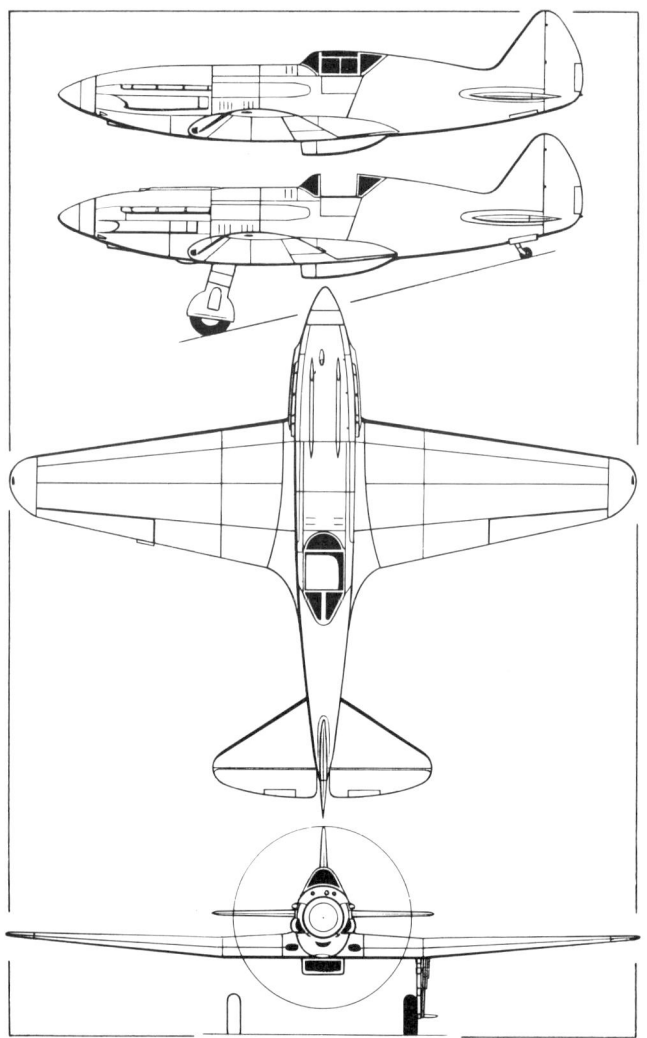

The side profile at the top of the above drawing illustrates a prototype MiG-1, the other views depicting the definitive production configuration

being imposed on its training organisation by a major expansion programme.

The MiG-3 had stemmed from one of the fighter requirements formulated by the UV-VS (Administration of the Air Forces) in 1938 and circulated to various experimental design bureaux on a competitive basis. This requirement called for a single-seat interceptor fighter offering maximum performance at altitudes above 19,685 ft (6 000 m), and contending design teams included that of OKB-155 headed by Artem I.Mikoyan and Mikhail I.Gurevich. Both Mikoyan and Gurevich had worked at the TsKB (Central Design Bureau) before joining forces to establish their own bureau, and the high-altitude fighter requirement particularly appealed to the former as it demanded an aircraft optimised for speed, this taking precedence over all other capabilities, whereas the parallel 'frontal' fighter requirement called for compromise, manoeuvrability being regarded as equal in importance to other aspects of the performance.

The Mikoyan-Gurevich OKB elected to utilise the AM-35A 12-cylinder liquid-cooled vee engine newly developed at the TsIAM (Central Institute of Aero Engine Construction) by a team led by Aleksandr Mikulin, whereas other contending designs (eg, Sukhoi Su-1) concentrated on a combination of the lighter Klimov-developed M-105 and TsIAM-developed turbo-superchargers. The AM-35A had a single-stage supercharger and afforded 1,350 hp at 2,050 rpm for take-off and maximum continuous ratings of 1,200 hp at 19,685 ft (6 000 m) and 1,150 hp at 22,965 ft (7 000 m). Unfortunately, the AM-35A was both a large and an extremely heavy engine; its dry weight of 1,830 lb (830 kg) compared unfavourably with the contemporary Rolls-Royce Merlin and Daimler-Benz DB 601A which had dry weights of 1,376 lb (624 kg) and 1,340 lb (608 kg) respectively.

The aim of the OKB was to design the smallest practical airframe capable of accommodating the AM-35A engine, a pilot and armament, and the weight of the power plant influenced the design of the fighter to a very marked degree. Structural weight had to be kept to a minimum in order to achieve an acceptable power-to-weight ratio — the problem posed by the overly heavy engine being compounded by the contemporary shortage of steel and light alloy which dictated extensive use of wood — and it was necessary to accommodate the pilot well aft in the fuselage for CG reasons.

The project was submitted to the GUAP (Chief Directorate of the Aviation Industry) late in 1938, and considered, together with competitive proposals, at a meeting held in the Kremlin in January 1939 (see page 9). Instructions to proceed with detail design as the I-20* were issued to the OKB shortly after this meeting,

existing and the building of new aircraft factories had been acted upon but none other than the Khodinka plant had achieved a sufficiently advanced stage in the production of a modern combat aircraft to create the impression that the Soviet government was anxious to impart. Furthermore, the MiG-3 was the only one of the V-VS's new-generation combat aircraft that could be displayed in adequately impressive numbers — no fewer than 1,269 MiG-3s were completed during the first six months of 1941 as compared with 677 examples of the Yak-1 and LaGG-3 combined.

The MiG-3 was, in fact, the first fighter of what had come to be considered the "modern formula" to be delivered to the V-VS in quantity, and the service had had some cause to believe that its progenitor, the MiG-1, was one of the fastest combat aircraft in production anywhere in the world. Its debut had represented a quantum leap in Soviet fighter performance, albeit one achieved at some cost to handling characteristics and manoeuvrability with a demand for a higher degree of pilot competence in consequence; a demand that the V-VS was finding difficulty in meeting owing to the strain

---

*The designation 'I-20' was to be supplanted by that of MiG-1 by the time the first prototype flew, but the OKB had adopted this as a bureau designation, adding a zero (ie, I-200) indicating the prototype status of the aeroplane and utilising a numerical sequence for subsequent designs (eg, I-210, I-220, I-230, etc), variations of the basic design being signified by the third digit (eg, I-211, I-212, etc).

The MiG-3-equipped 12 IAP receiving the Guards standard early in 1942 after distinguishing itself in action as a component of the Moscow PVO. MiG-3s of the 12 IAP are seen at the foot of the page

facilities being provided in *Zavod* 1 at Khodinka where detail design was completed during the following October, work on four prototypes commencing during the course of the following month. Before the first of these was completed, barely five months later, *Zavod* 1 had begun tooling for an initial batch of 100 examples of the new fighter, which had by now been designated MiG-1, the intention being to use these aircraft for simultaneous test programmes at several experimental centres as well as for service evaluation.

The new fighter comprised dural-skinned welded steel-tube forward and centre fuselage and a wooden

A considerable number of MiG-3s were damaged during the initial Luftwaffe onslaught on V-VS airfields and were subsequently captured by the advancing Wehrmacht, two of these being illustrated (above and left). The Luftwaffe held the MiG-3 in poor esteem owing to the inadequacy of its armament and relatively poor manoeuvrability, but the Soviet fighter was at a disadvantage at the altitudes that most combat took place

monocoque rear fuselage with bakelite ply skinning. The wing centre section was built integral with the centre fuselage and was of steel with dural skinning, while the outer panels were of laminated spruce with a single mainspar, two auxiliary spars and bakelite ply skinning. The integral vertical fin was of wooden construction and, like the dural tailplane, covered by bakelite ply, all movable control surfaces were metal framed and fabric skinned, and plain dural sheet split trailing-edge flaps were fitted. All three members of the undercarriage were retracted pneumatically, the main members, which had a track of 9 ft 1¼ in (2,80 m), folding inwards into wells in the wing centre section, forward of the fuel tanks. The AM-35A drove a VISh-22E metal three-bladed controllable-pitch propeller and provision was made for 89 Imp gal (404 l) of fuel which was distributed between a 23 Imp gal (109 l) fuselage tank and two 33 Imp gal (150 l) centre section tanks, these being protected by a sheathing of layers of tough cord fabric. The pilot was seated over the wing trailing edge, the cockpit being enclosed by a sideways-hinging canopy, and for a combination of CG and weight reasons, armament was restricted to a pair of 7,62-mm ShKAS machine guns with 375 rpg and a single 12,7-mm UB machine gun with 300 rounds, although this was not mounted by the first prototypes.

The first prototype MiG-1 made its initial test flight at Khodinka on 5 April 1940 with Arkadii N.Yekatov at the controls, and seven weeks later, on 24 May, Yekatov attained a speed of 403 mph (648,5 km/h) in level flight at an altitude of 22,640 ft (6 900 m). From the outset of flight testing, however, it was obvious that, while Mikoyan and Gurevich had achieved their primary aim of creating an exceptionally fast high-altitude fighter, they had done so at cost to all other characteristics. Smaller than the Spitfire but appreciably heavier, its wing loading without armament or other operational equipment being of the order of 35.8 lb/sq ft 175 kg/m²) the MiG-1 suffered extremely poor longitudinal stability; control response was sluggish under virtually all flight conditions; it had a tendency to enter a vicious spin from a sharp banking turn and its landing characteristics were considered to be such as to restrict the aircraft to only the most experienced of pilots.

It was obvious that some of the more fundamental shortcomings of the MiG-1 — such as the longitudinal instability which stemmed from the brevity of the rear fuselage — were inherent in the design. Engineering test pilots of the NII V-VS were responsible for performing the State Acceptance Trials of the MiG-1, and shortly before these began, Arkadii Yekatov lost his life when the AM-35A engine of his prototype MiG-1 failed during a landing approach. The NII V-VS pilot assigned the task of performing the initial flight testing of the official acceptance programme was Andrei G. Kotchetkov, who had been a fellow pupil of Artem Mikoyan at the Zhukovsky Air Force Engineering Academy. He performed the first flight test a few days after the accident in which Yekatov had been killed, and shortly after taking-off, the AM-35A engine failed. By an extraordinary feat of piloting, he completed a 180-degree turn and landed the aircraft successfully.

The State Acceptance Trials were completed in August 1940, and while the test pilots universally praised its speed and altitude performance, they were equally unanimous in their censure of the MiG-1's handling characteristics, manoeuvrability and stability. They were also critical of its range capability and substantial redesign was called for. By this time, the first series MiG-1s were nearing completion on the *Zavod* 1 assembly line, following on the last of the Polikarpov I-153 fighter biplanes that had been produced in the factory, and after consultation between the *Narkomavprom* (State Commissariat of the Aviation Industry), the NII V-VS and the TsAGI (Central Aero- and Hydrodynamic Institute), it was decided to complete the series of 100 aircraft laid down and, in the meantime, the Mikoyan-Gurevich OKB would undertake the necessary redesign to enhance the handling characteristics of the fighter and simultaneously improve its range capability. Two large wind tunnels, T 101 and T 104, had been placed in operation by the TsAGI late in 1939, and a full-scale tunnel programme was to be conducted in parallel with further trials at various test establishments with the aim of having an acceptable fighter embodying all necessary redesign and modification ready to follow on the last of the initial series of 100 aircraft early in 1941.

Meanwhile, more minor modifications were phased onto the *Zavod* 1 assembly line, these effectively slowing the delivery tempo and only 20 MiG-1s had been completed by the end of 1940, compared with more than three times that number scheduled. The production MiG-1 retained all the undesirable features of the

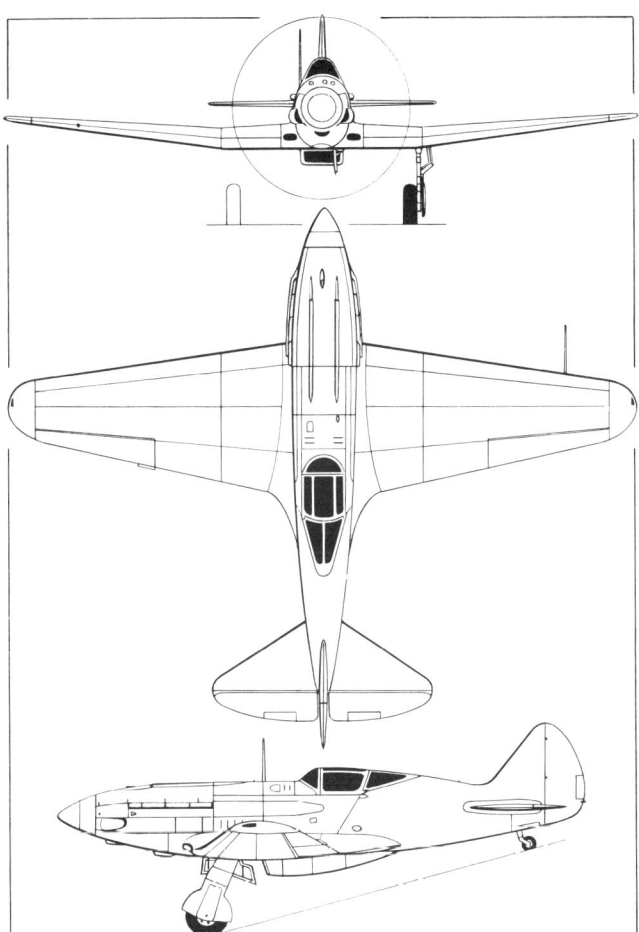

The three-view general arrangement drawing above depicts the standard production MiG-3

prototypes and low-speed characteristics had, in fact, worsened as a result of the addition of armament and an 8-mm armour plate behind the pilot's seat which raised the normal gross weight to 6,770 lb (3 071 kg) and wing loading to 36 lb/sq ft (176 kg/m²). The pilot was provided with a simple PBP-1 reflector sight, provision was made for an RSI-3 single-channel radio, although this was usually omitted, and instrumentation was strictly limited — neither gyroscopic instruments nor fuel gauge were fitted, the pilot having to attune his ear to the note of the engine to determine the fuel status.

The average V-VS pilot's predilection for an open cockpit was reflected by the deletion of the sideways-hinging canopy that had characterised the prototypes, but high-speed performance remained relatively spectacular, maximum speed ranging from 298 mph (480 km/h) at sea level to 363 mph (585 km/h) at 16,400 ft (5 000 m) and 375 mph (604 km/h) at 19,685 ft (6 000 m), while 390 mph (628 km/h) was attainable at 23,295 ft (7 100 m). An altitude of 16,400 ft (5 000 m) could be reached in 5.3 minutes and maximum ceiling was 39,370 ft (12 000 m), but the poorest aspect of the MiG-1's performance envelope was its range, which, with full tanks at long-range cruise, was only 454 miles (730 km). At maximum cruise of 342 mph (550 km/h) with 10 per cent fuel reserve for hold-off and landing, range was reduced to a mere 360 miles (580 km).

Early in 1941, the first MiG-1s were distributed to selected service units for evaluation and familiarisation, these units being components of the IAP-VO (*Istrebitelnaya aviatsiya protivo-vozdushnoi oborony* — Fighter Aviation of the Anti-aircraft Defence) assigned the task of defending primary targets, and of the V-VS VMF (*Voennomorskovo flota* — Air Forces of the Navy), the Baltic Fleet having priority. Only the most experienced of their pilots were assigned to the MiG-1 and even these found it a very exacting machine to fly. Forward view for taxying and take-off was virtually non-existent; the fighter was extremely unwieldy at lower speeds and altitudes; controls were heavy at the upper end of the speed range and extreme caution had to be exercised during aerobatics and landing as the MiG-1 still retained the predilection for spinning out of a steep banking turn that had been displayed during the flight-testing of the prototypes.

With the MiG-1, the phenomena of the high-speed stall was encountered by V-VS pilots for the first time, necessitating careful practice of turns at varying speeds and rates of turn to accustom them to the symptoms of an approaching stall. It was hardly to be expected that such characteristics, coupled with a strictly limited endurance and what was already considered inadequate armament, would endear the MiG fighter to the V-VS and its service introduction could, at best, be described as an inauspicious success.

Tunnel testing and the results of trials and service evaluation were meanwhile being fed back to the Mikoyan-Gurevich OKB at Khodinka and resulting in a variety of changes and modifications. The wing structure was revised and increased dihedral was applied to the outer panels; the supercharger air intake was redesigned and cut back and the ventral radiator

The MiG-3 was the most prolific of V-VS fighters during the first winter of the German attack on the Soviet Union, but their effectiveness was strictly limited by the requirements of the specification to which they had been designed. Many were assigned to the tactical reconnaissance role and for the intercept task they were largely restricted to the defence of specific targets. Here MiG-3s are seen operating from snow-covered bases in the winter of 1941-42

MiG-3s of the 34 IAP operating from Vnukovo, Moscow, during the winter of 1941-42. The legend beneath the cockpit of the aircraft in the foreground reads "For the Fatherland", other patriotic inscriptions appearing on the aircraft in the background

bath was enlarged and extended forward; a cockpit canopy was reintroduced, this being of entirely new design and sliding aft and the fuselage decking was cut down at a more acute angle and glazed to improve aft vision; the hinged lower halves of the mainwheel cover plates were removed from the main covers and transferred to the fuselage, and a 54 Imp gal (245 l) overload fuel tank was introduced beneath the pilot's seat.

These and various other refinements were embodied by the 101st production fighter which came off the Khodinka assembly line in February 1941, the modified variant being redesignated officially as the MiG-3. Overall performance had been marginally improved, the additional fuel tank had augmented range and endurance to an acceptable degree, stability had been decidedly improved, as were also the control forces, and by general consensus, the handling characteristics were now acceptable, although it was tacitly admitted that the MiG-3 was no novice's aeroplane and, while a major improvement on the MiG-1, it called for a high degree of piloting skill. Weight had become an increasingly critical factor, however, and although the empty weight of 5,950 lb (2 699 kg) revealed an increase of only some 88 lb (40 kg) over that of the MiG-1, take-off weight in clean condition with maximum fuel had risen to 7,385 lb (3 350 kg), and the admittedly inadequate armament had perforce remained unchanged in order to avoid yet further weight escalation.

Such had been the impetus placed behind the production programme that the first MiG-3s began to reach the IAPs during the course of March 1941, and a second factory had completed tooling and was about to supplement the output of *Zavod* 1 at the time of the previously-mentioned German delegation's visit, when output tempo of the fighter was approaching 75 aircraft per week — both Artem Mikoyan and Mikhail Gurevich received the coveted title of "Stalin Prize Laureate" for their efforts in organising the volume production of the warplane in record time.

The regiments possessing a high proportion of experienced pilots, such as those of the IA-PVO which had enjoyed a higher standard of training, accepted more readily the idiosyncracies of the MiG-3 than did the average fighter regiment, which was manned by poorly-trained pilots who had logged only between 50 and 90 hours flying per year since gaining their wings. To the latter, the advent of the MiG-3 posed many problems. A former NII V-VS engineering test pilot, Pyotr M.Stefanovsky, was later to relate how, in May 1941, he received instructions to proceed immediately to Kishinev in Moldavia, near the Rumanian border, where an *IA Divisiya* — Fighter Aviation Division — commanded by Gen.Osipenko was apparently reluctant to relinquish its I-153s and I-16s in favour of the more advanced fighter. The Division was the first to receive a full complement of MiG-3s and possessed two full sets of fighters, its older Polikarpov types and a similar number of the Mikoyan-Gurevich fighter, yet not one pilot had attempted to fly the new warplane, believing it to possess decidedly lethal propensities. The conversion of the *Divisiya* was considered a matter of the utmost urgency, but none of its pilots evinced any enthusiasm to undertake a familiarisation flight in the MiG-3 until Stefanovsky took one of the fighters into the air and demonstrated its capabilities.

Among the first regiments to convert to the MiG-3 was the 55 IAP, which was destined to be the first unit equipped with this fighter to see combat, the crack 16 Guards IAP, the 1 Guards IAP which was assigned to

(Opposite page) A MiG-3 at an advanced airfield in the central sector in the summer of 1942. (Above) An unserviceable MiG-3 abandoned by the V-VS at an airfield overrun by the Wehrmacht and (below right) a MiG-3 of the 12 Guards IAP with RS-82 rockets

the Northern Fleet and the 32 IAP assigned to the Black Sea Fleet. Many MiG-3s were assigned to regiments defending the major centres of industry, such as the 34 IAP and the 233 IAP which formed component parts of the Moscow PVO, the former, commanded by Major Leonid G.Rybkin, operating from the southern side of the Vnukovo airfield and the latter, commanded by Major Konstantin M.Kuzmenko, being based at Tushino. Shortly before the German assault on the Soviet Union began, two volunteer regiments, the 401 and 402 IAPs, were formed on MiG-3s, primarily with test pilots from the NII V-VS, these being commanded by Lt.Col.Stepan P.Suprun and Lt.Col.Pyotr M.Stefanovsky respectively.

The 401 IAP, with its highly-experienced pilots, achieved some success during the first weeks of the German attack, although its CO, Stepan Suprun* was killed on 4 July 1941 while flying from an airfield near Borisov. Several of the leading V-VS aces were to gain their first "kills" while flying the MiG-3, such as the second top-scoring Soviet fighter pilot, Aleksandr I.Pokryshkin, who gained his first victory on 23 June, the second day of the German assault. Flying with 55 IAP, Pokryshkin shot down a Bf 109E of JG 77 near Jassy while engaged in escorting a formation of Tupolev SB bombers. Some months later, on 20 November, he discovered Gen. Paul von Kleist's Panzer Group approaching Rostov in a snowstorm while flying a voluntary tactical reconnaissance mission in a

MiG-3. Other leading V-VS fighter pilots who did well while flying the MiG-3 included Capt.Aleksandr F.Klubov of the 16 Guards IAP, who converted to the Mikoyan-Gurevich fighter after flying I-153 biplanes operationally, once taking on six Bf 109s single-handed and shooting down two of them, his MiG-3 emerging unscathed from the conflict. Dmitri B.Glinka, who was to be credited with a similar score (ie, 50 'kills') to that of Klubov, also flew the MiG-3 for a period. These were the exceptions, however, for few of the IAPs that had received the MiG-3 by the time the *Wehrmacht* launched Operation *Barbarossa* were thoroughly versed in the characteristics of their new mount.

The *Luftwaffe* fighter pilots reported that, in general, the MiG-3 units appeared singularly lacking in aggressiveness. This was partly due to the inexperience and inadequate training of the average V-VS pilot, but there was also a more cogent reason: tacit admission that the MiG-3, optimised for the high-altitude role, was at a distinct disadvantage in fighter-versus-fighter combat with the Messerschmitt Bf 109 below 19,685 ft (6 000 m) and virtually all combat took place below this altitude. Thus, the MiG-3 pilots

---

Suprun was the first V VS pilot of WW II to be pronounced Hero of the Soviet Union for the second time, being first accorded this distinction in 1940 for his flight test work with the Polikarpov I-180 and the Yak-1 fighters, and posthumously on 22 July 1941. Command of the 401 IAP was then taken over by V.V.Kokkinaki who remained CO until the test pilots were recalled to the NII V-VS, the regiment having claimed 54 'kills' over a period of three months.

usually attempted to avoid combat with enemy single-seaters, concentrating on the interception of bombers and reconnaissance aircraft, although, in this task the excellent speed capability of the Mikoyan-Gurevich fighter was in part counterbalanced by the inadequacy of its firepower. This led to several attempts in the field to improve armament effectiveness, the most commonly adopted being the attachment of six RS-82 rocket missiles beneath the wings* and a less official modification being the attachment of a pair of 12,7-mm UB machine guns beneath the wings**. With such supplementary weapons, loaded weight rose as high as 7,705 lb (3 495 kg) and frequently the standard RSI-3 or -4 radio and even the cockpit canopy were discarded as contributions towards resolving the critical weight problem. A 20-mm ShVAK cannon was experimentally fitted between the cylinder banks of the engine (AM-35P), but this development was abandoned for reasons of weight.

Apart from inadequate firepower and the fact that it was a difficult aircraft to master, the principal shortcoming of the MiG-3 was not an inherent design fault; it was simply that necessity dictated its assignment to combat under conditions for which it had never been intended. Thus, with the availability of increasing numbers of LaGG-1s and Yak-1s, the MiG-3 was progressively withdrawn from the 'frontal' fighter role to which it had been largely committed owing to the exigencies of the times and was reassigned to IA-PVO units, such as the 12 Guards IAP in the western sector of the Moscow PVO which exchanged its Yak-1s for MiG-3s — it was the fact that this regiment distinguished itself in combat with the MiG-3 that resulted in its award of the coveted "Guards" title in 1942.

From the early weeks of the conflict, it became painfully obvious that the specialised high-altitude interceptor as epitomised by the MiG-3 was a luxury that the Soviet Union could ill afford at that stage of the war. Virtually all aerial combat was taking place at altitudes at which the MiG-3 was decidedly at a disadvantage, and with the transfer of the bulk of the Soviet aircraft industry eastward, coupled with a demand to reduce the number of individual aircraft types to which the industry was committed, plus the higher priority that was being placed on the low-altitude AM-38 engine for the Il-2 *shturmovik* which could only be produced at the expense of the MiG-3's high-altitude AM-35A, the decision was taken to phase out the MiG-3 at the earliest opportunity. The *Zavod* 1 was evacuated from Khodinka to Kuibyshev, but production of the MiG-3 finally terminated in the spring of 1942, when a total of 3,322 fighters of this type had been delivered. At that time development was still proceeding of the MiG-3D which was to be powered by the Mikulin AM-39 engine, which, rated at 1,700 hp, was still at a relatively early stage in its test programme. The MiG-3D was eventually to be flown by Yu.A.Antipov and was to be pronounced an excellent high-altitude fighter, but as there was little likelihood of the AM-39 becoming available in production quantities in the short term, the MiG-3D served primarily as a development aircraft for the longer-term I-220 and I-230 series fighters.

The end of production did not, of course, signify the early demise of the MiG-3 in V-VS service. Numerically it was to remain an important aircraft in the fighter inventory for a further two years, being employed primarily for rear area defence, having been progressively withdrawn from the fighter units assigned to the more important PVO regions from early 1943. During this time, a number of modifications were tested with a view to improving specific aspects of the fighter's performance, some of these modifications being applied retrospectively to service MiG-3s, and between 1942 and 1944, maximum speed was raised by 30 mph (50 km/h) at sea level by uprating the engine. One modified version in which take-off weight was raised to 8,818 lb (4 000 kg) by the introduction of overload fuel tanks as the MiG-3DD (*Dalny deistvya* indicating extended range) was tested in the early months of 1944 but was not adopted, this apparently being a modification of one of the MiG-3D prototypes with the AM-39 engine.

MiG-3 Specification
Power Plant: One Mikulin AM-35A 12-cylinder Vee liquid-cooled engine rated at 1,350 hp at 2,050 rpm for take-off, 1,200 hp at 2,050 rpm at 19,685 ft (6 000 m) and 1,150 hp at 2,050 rpm at 22,965 ft (7 000 m), driving a 9 ft 10 in (3,00 m) diam VISh-61Shch three-blade constant-speed metal propeller. Total fuel capacity of 143 Imp gal (650 l) distributed between two wing centre section and two fuselage tanks.
Performance: Max speed, 298 mph (480 km/h) at sea level, 312 mph (503 km/h) at 3,280 ft (1 000 m), 325 mph (523 km/h) at 6,560 ft (2 000 m), 338 mph (544 km/h) at 9,840 ft (3 000 m), 351 mph (565 km/h) at 13,125 ft (4 000 m), 363 mph (585 km/h) at 16,405 ft (5 000 m), 375 mph (604 km/h) at 19,685 ft (6 000 m), 388 mph (625 km/h) at 22,965 ft (7 000 m), 398 mph (640 km/h) at 25,590 ft (7 800 m); econ cruise, 280 mph (450 km/h); max continuous cruise, 342 mph (550 km/h); range at long-range cruise at 16,400 ft (5 000 m), 777 mls (1 250 km), at max continuous cruise with 10% reserve, 510 mls (820 km); time to 16,400 ft (5 000 m), 5.7 min; ceiling, 39,370 ft (12 000 m).
Weights: Empty equipped, 5,950 lb (2 699 kg); normal loaded, 7,385 lb (3 350 kg).
Dimensions: Span, 33 ft 9½ in (10,30 m); length, 26 ft 8⅞ in (8,15 m); height, 8 ft 7⅛ in (2,62 m); wing area, 187.72 sq ft (17,44 m^2).
Armament: Two 7,62-mm Shpital'ny-Komaritsky ShKAS machine guns with 375 rpg and one 12,7-mm Berezin UB machine gun with 300 rounds. Provision for external as six 82-mm RS-82 rockets.

These missiles were intended for use in air-to-air combat and not, as has been suggested by some sources, to endow the MiG-3 with a secondary ground attack capability.

**Pyotr Stefanovsky relates in his memoirs an incident in which a pilot of 401 IAP, V.I.Khomyakov, was flying a MiG-3 which had been unofficially modified to take an additional pair of UB machine guns early in July 1941. Flying as part of a formation of five MiG-3s, Khomyakov could not keep up with his companions owing to the increased weight and drag of the additional armament. When he returned to base, he discovered that two of the formation of MiG-3s to which he had been attached had been lost and he was promptly confined in the local military prison on a charge of negligence.*

MIKOYAN-GUREVICH DIS

Although the twin-engined single-seat fighter concept saw birth late in World War I, it failed to achieve vogue until the mid 'forties. In the intervening years, desultory consideration was given to such warplanes in most of the major aircraft-manufacturing countries and the Soviet Union was no exception, the UV-VS (Administration of the Air Forces) formulating a requirement for a long-range single-seat twin-engined escort fighter in 1939, and OKB-155 successfully tendering a proposal referred to simply as the DIS (*Dvukhmotorny istrebitel soprovozhdenya* — Twin-engined Escort Fighter).

A low-wing cantilever monoplane primarily of wooden construction, the DIS followed the formula established by Artem Mikoyan and Mikhail Gurevich in representing the smallest practicable airframe that could accommodate the pilot, the specified armament, the selected engines and sufficient fuel to meet the somewhat exacting range demand. The fuselage, which was an oval-section monocoque with *delta-drevesina* (delta timber) longerons, birch frames and bakelite ply skinning, featured an abbreviated nose which barely extended beyond the wing leading edge, accommodated the pilot over the wing centre section and was intended to mount a 37-mm Shpital'ny-Komaritsky cannon beneath the cockpit. The two-spar wing was of broad chord, featured marked leading-edge taper and was built in three sections, the centre section, which was built integral with the fuselage, being exceptionally thick and embodying marked anhedral. The upper portion of the wing centre section housed four 7,62-mm ShKAS machine guns. The main fuel tanks were also accommodated in the centre section, with small supplementary tanks aft of the pilot and outboard of the engine nacelles. The wing structure was built up on *delta-drevesina* box spars and had similar skinning to that of the fuselage. The engines, the nacelles of which projected well forward of the fuselage nose and provided bays for the aft-retracting main undercarriage members, were Mikulin AM-37s, these 12-cylinder vee liquid-cooled units being rated at 1,400 hp for take-off and 1,300 hp at rated altitude.

Although designed primarily for the escort role, the DIS had the secondary roles of ground attack and torpedo-bombing for which up to 1,764 lb (800 kg) of bombs could be carried by underwing racks or a single torpedo beneath the fuselage. Provision was also made for the installation of reconnaissance cameras. At least two prototypes of the DIS were completed by *Zavod* 1 at Khodinka during the late spring and early summer of 1941. Loaded weight was 17,770 lb (8 060 kg) and estimated performance included a maximum speed of 379 mph (610 km/h), a range of 1,417 miles (2 280 km), the ability to climb to 16,400 ft (5 000 m) in 5.5 min and a ceiling of 35,760 ft (10 900 m).

The need for aircraft of the DIS category was by no means universally acknowledged and it was considered in some quarters that single-seat long-range escort fighters were a luxury that the V-VS, which was essentially tactically orientated, could ill afford. Furthermore, the Mikoyan-Gurevich OKB was heavily committed to the improvement of the MiG-3 then entering service in quantity, and the DIS was thus allocated relatively low development priority. Difficulties were encountered with the AM-37 engines and relatively limited flight testing had been conducted when the OKB was transferred from Khodinka to Kuibyshev in the autumn of 1941. Nevertheless, development of the basic design was continued and a revised version was tested in 1942.

The developed version of the DIS differed from the initial model primarily in having two Shvetsov M-82F 14-cylinder radial air-cooled engines each rated at 1,700 hp for take-off and driving four-blade propellers. The engines were close-cowled and their nacelles were extended aft of the wing trailing edges. The fuselage

Although no photographs of the original DIS twin-engined escort fighter are available, these photographs of a model of the initial version give some impression of the various innovative design features that it embodied, noteworthy being the abbreviated fuselage nose and the deep-section broad-chord reverse gull wing

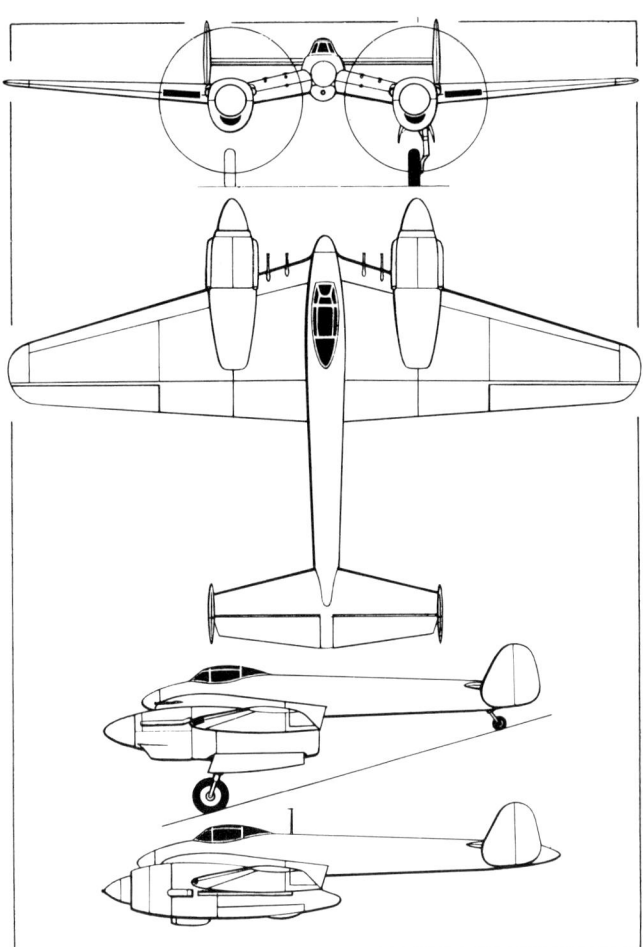

remained essentially unchanged, although the nose section was marginally lengthened and the tailcone was extended aft of the horizontal surfaces. The quartet of 7,62-mm ShKAS machine guns was transferred from the wing centre section to the fuselage nose where they were joined by two 23-mm Volkov-Yartsev VYa-23V cannon which supplanted the single 37-mm ShK weapon. Several prototypes of the M-82F-powered DIS were completed at Kuibyshev and State Acceptance Trials were performed successfully, plans being formulated for series production as the MiG-5. However, V-VS bombing operations were largely restricted to the tactical role and it was concluded that existing 'frontal' fighters were adequate to provide any necessary escort for such missions. Thus, the MiG-5 production programme was abandoned and further development of the DIS was discontinued late in 1942.

DIS Specification
Power Plant: Two Shvetsov M-82F 14-cylinder radial air-cooled engines each rated at 1,700 hp at 2,400 rpm for take-off, 1,540 hp at 2,400 rpm at 6,725 ft (2 050 m) and 1,330 hp at 17,715 ft (5 400 m), driving four-blade constant-speed propellers.
Performance: Max speed, 375 mph (604 km/h) at 22,965 ft (7 000 m); max range, 1,553 mls (2 500 km) at long-range cruise; time to 16,400 ft (5 000 m), 6.3 min; ceiling, 32,150 ft (9 800 m).
Weights: No details available.
Dimensions: No details available other than wing area of 418.72 sq ft (38,90 m²).
Armament: Four 7,62-mm Shpital'ny-Komaritsky ShKAS machine guns and two 23-mm Volkov-Yartsev VYa-23V cannon in forward fuselage.

The general arrangement drawing (above left) depicts the original AM-37-powered DIS, the lower sideview illustrating the M-82F-engined development for comparison purposes. The latter is also illustrated below and several prototypes of the radial engined version performed State Acceptance Trials during the course of 1942

MIKOYAN-GUREVICH I-211

The successful mating of an air-cooled radial engine to a single-seat fighter airframe designed from the outset for a liquid-cooled inline engine represents no mean feat of engineering and World War II was to witness singularly few such metamorphoses achieve production status. One such, the Japanese Kawasaki Ki.100, which appeared early in 1945, was purely the result of *force majeure* — no alternative to an air-cooled radial presenting itself as a successor to the liquid-cooled inline unit that was no longer available. In the Soviet Union, on the other hand, a concerted effort was made to adapt existing inline-engined fighter airframes for an air-cooled radial as a safeguard against any shortages of the inline units for which the fighters had been conceived. The engine prompting this programme was the 14-cylinder two-row M-82 radial, which, developed by Arkadii D.Shvetsov's bureau, had successfully completed its State Acceptance Trials and had been placed in production in May 1941. The M-82 was rated at 1,700 hp at 2,400 rpm for take-off, nominal power being 1,540 hp at 6,725 ft (2 050 m), and its dry weight was 1,874 lb (850 kg).

In the case of the Mikoyan-Gurevich OKB, instructions to investigate the possibilities of adapting the MiG-3 airframe to take the M-82 radial had particular significance in that it had already been informed that the Mikulin AM-35A liquid-cooled engine powering the fighter was to be withdrawn from production by the end of 1941 owing to the production priority allocated to the low-altitude AM-38 for the Il-2 *shturmovik*. Thus, the OKB initiated the design of a conversion to take the new power plant primarily with the view to prolonging the production life of the basic airframe.

The M-82 weighed only 44 lb (20 kg) more than the AM-35A that it was to replace, this being appreciably less than the weight of the coolant system demanded by the Mikulin engine, and thus no serious CG shift had to be catered for. However, the radial engine was 15 in (38,50 cm) wider than the inline unit and while the substantial increase in drag in which this inevitably resulted was mitigated by use of a propeller extension shaft and a close-fitting Mercier-style cowling, which restored fineness ratio to a figure closely comparable to that of the standard MiG-3, the wind tunnel testing of models of the proposed M-82-powered fighter — which had been assigned the OKB designation I-210 — during the summer of 1941 produced disappointing results, drag proving markedly higher than predicted. Some minor changes were introduced on the prototype conversion as a result of the wind tunnel results, engine air intake area being reduced — front and rear fans were provided and it was believed that engine cooling would still be adequate while a considerable saving in drag could be effected — and the carburettor and supercharger intake trunking being led forward to the upper lip of the intake, and in this form, as the I-211, the prototype was flown for the first time in late August 1941.

Virtually identical to the standard MiG-3 aft of the engine firewall and carrying an armament of two 12,7-mm Berezin UB and two 7,62-mm Shpital'ny-Komaritsky ShKAS machine guns in the forward fuselage firing through long blast tubes arranged symmetrically around the engine cowling, the I-211 revealed that, despite a marginally lower normal all-up weight and the substantial increase in power provided by the M-82 engine, it was some 10 per cent slower than the MiG-3 above 16,405 ft (5 000 m), maximum attainable speed being 351 mph (565 km/h) at 20,180 ft (6 150 m), and at such speeds tail buffeting became so severe that the aircraft was barely controllable. Furthermore, all the least desirable handling characteristics of the AM-35A-powered fighter were accentuated by the I-211. The prototype was, therefore, promptly transferred to the full-scale TsAGI wind tunnel in which it was ascertained that turbulence generated immediately aft of the engine cowling was responsible for the buffeting.

The side profile immediately below illustrates the I-211, the lower side profile, the plan and head-on views depicting the I-211(Ye)

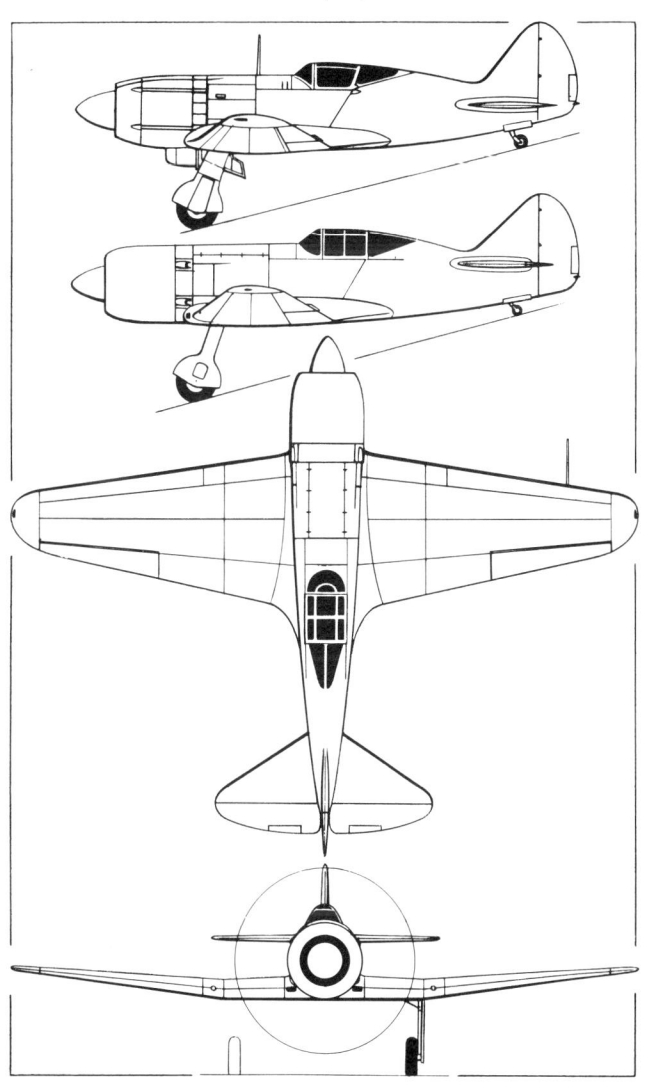

The Mikoyan-Gurevich OKB at once began reworking the design, a process interrupted by its transfer to Kuibyshev, but a revised prototype, the I-211(Ye) — the 'Ye' suffix indicating *Yedinitsa* which may be literally translated as 'Single Unit', in other words, a 'one-off' aircraft — was readied for testing in the late spring of 1942. In the development of this, the OKB had the benefit of the close co-operation of Arkadii Shvetsov's engine bureau in evolving an entirely new cowling for the M-82. An extremely clean, tapered cowling, entirely devoid of excrescencies enclosed an improved M-82F (ASh-82F) engine. The separate exhaust outlet gills were discarded and the exhaust pipes were clustered together (seven per side) in a similar fashion to those of the BMW 801 installation on the Fw 190, ejecting through vertical louvres, the supercharger and oil cooler intakes being transferred to the wing roots. Armament was removed from the fuselage, two wing-mounted 20-mm ShVAK cannon being substituted; some structural redesign of the centre fuselage was introduced; the cockpit canopy was raised to improve the pilot's view; the horizontal tail surfaces were repositioned higher on the fuselage and new, longer-stroke main undercarriage units were adopted.

The I-211(Ye) displayed markedly improved characteristics over those of its predecessor during the flight test programme which continued throughout the summer of 1942 and in the course of which the fuel-injection FN version of the engine replaced the M-82F, a maximum level speed of 416 mph (670 km/h) being achieved in level flight at 16,405 ft (5 000 m). Consideration was given to the series production of the I-211(Ye) but the similarly-powered and armed La-5 had already achieved quantity production, and the Mikoyan-Gurevich fighter, while marginally faster, possessed inferior manoeuvrability. Furthermore, while the I-211(Ye) retained much of the structure of the MiG-3, the AM-35A-powered fighter had already been phased out of production. Therefore, the further development of the I-211(Ye) was discontinued.

I-211(Ye) specification

Power Plant: One Shvetsov M-82FN (ASh-82FN) 14-cylinder two-row radial air-cooled engine rated at 1,850 hp at 2,500 rpm (for two minutes) for take-off, 1,650 hp at 2,400 rpm at 5,415 ft (1 650 m) and 1,450 hp at 2,400 rpm at 15,255 ft (4 650 m), driving a VISh-105V three-bladed controllable-pitch metal propeller of 9.84 ft (3,00 m) diam.
Performance: Max speed, 416 mph (670 km/h) at 16,405 ft (5 000 m); max range, 708 mls (1 140 km); time to 16,405 ft (5 000 m), 4.0 min; service ceiling, 37,075 ft (11 300 m).
Weights: Normal loaded, 7,407 lb (3 360 kg).
Dimensions: Span, 33 ft 9½ in (10,30 m); length, 26 ft 0 in (7,92 m); height, 8 ft 6 in (2,59 m); wing area, 187.72 sq ft (17,44 m²).
Armament: Two 20-mm Shpital'ny-Vladimirov ShVAK cannon mounted in wings.

(Above) The I-211 seen in the background of a propaganda photograph but showing the close-fitting Mercier-style cowling initially tested, and (below) the extensively revised I-211 (Ye) with entirely new engine cowling, redesigned centre fuselage and repositioned horizontal tail surfaces

MIKOYAN-GUREVICH I-220 (SERIES)

Despite the pressing need for low- to medium-altitude 'frontal' fighters in 1941, the development of more specialised high-altitude fighters was not entirely neglected and during the summer of that year, the Mikoyan-Gurevich OKB launched the development of two such warplanes in parallel, these being intended as successors to the MiG-3. Assigned the design bureau designations I-220 and I-230, the two aircraft had many common features. Both were intended for Aleksandr Mikulin's AM-39 12-cylinder liquid-cooled vee engine, other common features being the long-span wing, the tail assembly and the undercarriage, and as originally conceived, the I-220 was the more advanced, longer-term development in that, unlike the I-230, it embodied turbo-superchargers and a pressurized cockpit.

The first I-220 series prototype, the I-220(A), began its flight test programme late in 1942, and was powered by an AM-39 engine driving a large-diameter propeller with four paddle blades, but was essentially an airframe test vehicle in that it was fitted with neither pressurised cockpit nor turbo-superchargers. Of similar overall configuration to the MiG-3, the I-220(A) was also of mixed construction, with a dural-covered welded steel-tube forward and centre fuselage, a wooden monocoque rear fuselage with bakelite ply skinning, and a three-piece wing with steel main and auxiliary spars and spruce ribs in the outer panels. Provision was made for an armament of two fuselage-mounted 20-mm ShVAK cannon. During flight testing early in 1943, the I-220(A) recorded a speed of 433 mph (697 km(h) at 25,590 ft (7800 m).

The second prototype, the I-221(2A) joined the flight test programme during the early summer of 1943, this having an AM-39A engine fitted with a pair of TsIAM-developed TK-2B turbo-superchargers. Testing of the I-221(2A) continued throughout 1943, being punctuated by failure of one or both turbo-superchargers, flight time also being restricted by the low reliability of the insufficiently-developed AM-39 engine, and it was not until February 1944 that the first definitive prototype, the I-222(3A) with both turbo-superchargers and cockpit pressurization, became available for flight testing.

The I-222(3A) was powered by an AM-39B-1 engine fitted with two TK-300B turbo-superchargers and had 1,630 hp available for take-off and 1,900 hp at rated altitude. The cockpit was constructed of welded duralumin sheet and was air conditioned and pressurized by air tapped from the compressor, a sandwich-type windscreen being provided and an inflatable rubber tube sealing the canopy. Plans were formulated for the series production of the I-222(3A) as the MiG-7, but, in the event, teething troubles still being suffered by the AM-39 engine, of which only a small pre-series had been produced, and the continuing poor reliability of the turbo-superchargers, coupled with the fact that the course of the war had virtually eliminated the threat of high altitude attack that the fighter had been evolved to counter, motivated against production proceeding. Nevertheless, two further I-220 series prototypes which had reached an advanced stage in construction were completed primarily for pressure cabin and turbo-supercharger development, and these, the I-224(4A) and I-225(5A), were both to lay claim to some distinction.

(At head of page and below) The I-224(4A) was one of the definitive developments in the I-220 series of high-altitude interceptors and, during the course of testing, achieved the greatest altitude reached by any Soviet piston-engined fighter

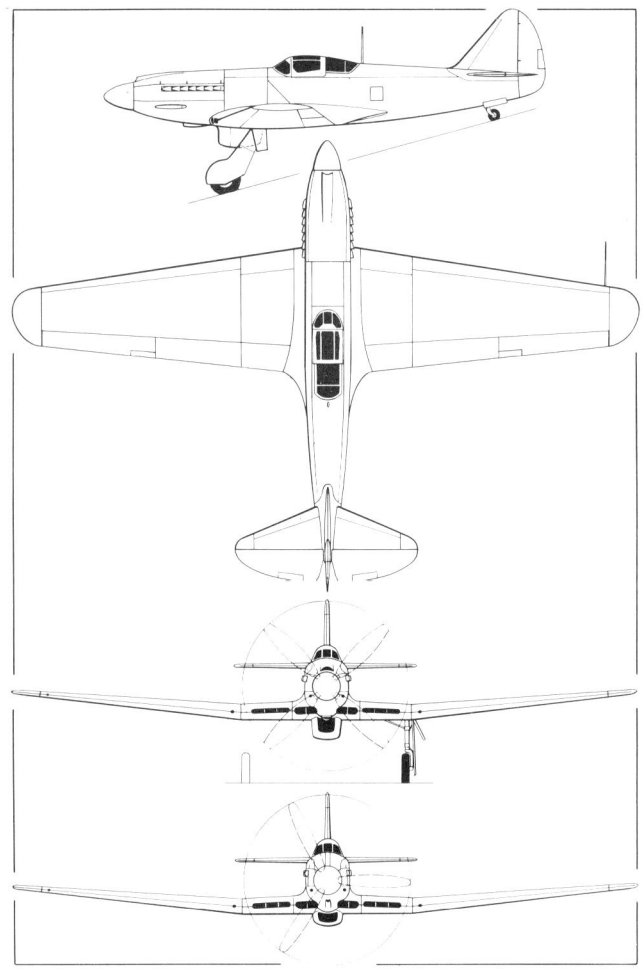

The I-224(4A), which was tested during the summer of 1944, was generally similar to its immediate predecessor, but was fitted with the slightly more powerful AM-39FB engine. During the course of its trials, this prototype was to achieve an altitude of 46,260 ft (14 100 m), the greatest height attained by any Soviet piston-engined fighter. The I-225(5A) differed principally in having an AM-42FB, the last of the Mikulin-developed series of 12-cylinder liquid-cooled vee engines, this having an output of 2,200 hp at rated altitude and driving a three-bladed propeller. Flown in March 1945, the I-225(5A) achieved a speed of 451 mph (726 km/h) at 32,810 ft (10 000 m), the highest speed ever to be attained in level flight by a Soviet piston-engined aircraft unassisted by any form of auxiliary power unit.

I-220 (Series) Specification
Power Plant: One Mikulin AM-39A, (I-222) AM-39B-1, (I-224) AM-39FB, or (I-225) AM-42FB 12-cylinder vee liquid-cooled engine rated at 1,700 hp, (AM-39B-1) 1,900 hp, (AM-39FB) 2,000 hp, or (AM-42FB) 2,200 hp at rated altitude with (I-221) two TK-2B or (I-222, -224 and -225) TK-300B turbo-superchargers.
Performance: Max speed (I-220), 433 mph (697 km/h) at 25,590 ft (7 800 m), (I-222), 429 mph (691 km/h) at 42,980 ft (13 100 m), (I-225), 451 mph (726 km/h) at 32,810 ft (10 000 m); ceiling (I-222), 45,930 ft (14 000 m), (I-224), 462,260 ft (14 100 m).
Weights: Normal loaded (I-222), 8,267 lb (3 750 kg), (I-224), 8,113 lb (3 780 kg).
Dimensions: Span, 42, 7⅘ in (13,00 m); length, 30 ft 2⅕ in (9,20 m); height, 11 ft 6⅕ in (3,51 m); wing area, 241.11 sq ft (22,40 m²).
Armament: Two or four 20-mm ShVAK cannon in fuselage nose.

The side profile, planview and upper head-on view (above left) depict the I-224 and the lower head-on view illustrates the I-225(5A) which is also depicted by the photograph below. The I-225(5A) reached the highest level-flight speed ever attained by any Soviet piston-engined fighter

(Above and below right) The I-231(2D), the second I-230 series prototype, was a rather less sophisticated high-altitude fighter than the parallel I-220 series and had closer afinity with the MiG-3

MIKOYAN-GUREVICH I-230

A parallel development to the previously-described I-220 and possessing many common features, the I-230 single-seat high-altitude fighter was somewhat less advanced in concept in that no provision was made for cockpit pressurization or turbo-supercharging and being, to all intents and purposes, a back-up programme to safeguard against undue delays in bringing to acceptable service standards the more innovative aspects of the I-220.

Employing an essentially similar airframe to that of the I-220, but lacking the cut-down rear fuselage and all-round vision cockpit canopy, the I-230 was aerodynamically an extremely clean design and commenced its flight test programme in the spring of 1942, at which time, owing to non-availability of a flight-cleared Mikulin AM-39 engine with which it was intended to power the fighter and which was at that time under test in the experimental MiG-3D, the prototype was fitted with the lower-powered AM-35A similar to that installed in the standard MiG-3. This prototype, the I-230(D), carried an armament of two fuselage-mounted 7,62-mm ShKAS machine guns and two wing-mounted 20-mm ShVAK cannon. Owing to the protracted teething troubles suffered by the AM-39 engine, the second I-230 series prototype, the I-231(2D), did not commence its flight test programme until the spring of 1943. The two fuselage-mounted machine guns were omitted, armament being restricted to the wing-mounted cannon.

Powered by a 1,700 hp AM-39 engine, the I-231(D) displayed excellent speed capability during its trials when 439 mph (707 km/h) was achieved at 23,295 ft (7 100 m), but by this time, development of the parallel I-220 series of pressurized turbo-supercharged fighters had progressed sufficiently to warrant discontinuation of the I-230 series as a back-up and, in consequence, the latter was abandoned.

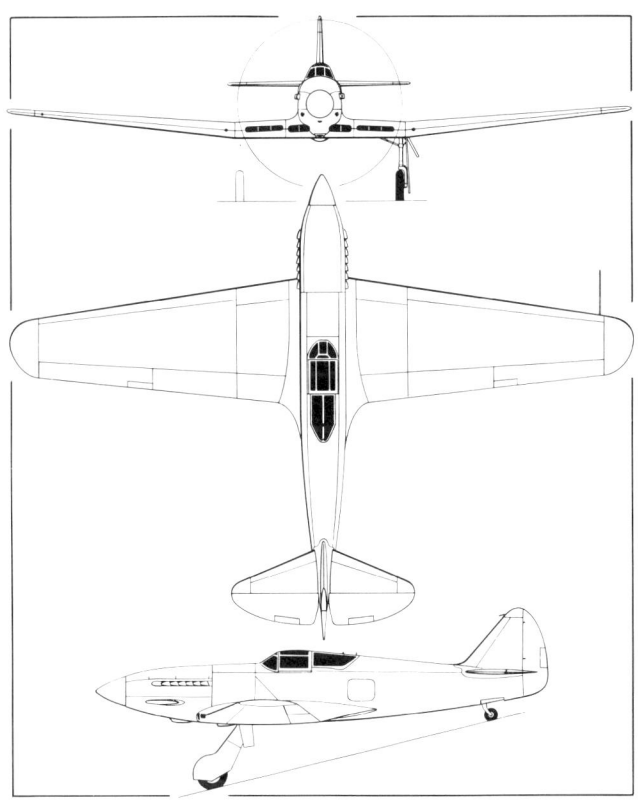

I-230 (Series) Specification
Power Plant: (I-231) One Mikulin AM-39 12-cylinder vee liquid-cooled engine rated at 1,580 hp for take-off and 1,700 hp at rated altitude and driving a three-blade constant-speed propeller.
Performance: Max speed, 439 mph (707 km/h) at 23,295 ft (7 100 m).
Weights: No details available.
Dimensions: Span, 42 ft 7⁴/₅ in (13,00 m); length, 31 ft 2 in (9,50 m); height, 11 ft 1⁴/₅ in (3,40 m); wing area, 241. 11 sq ft (22,40 m²).
Armament: Two 20-mm Shpital'ny-Vladimirov ShVAK cannon mounted in wings.

MIKOYAN-GUREVICH I-250(N)

Following Soviet receipt of intelligence reports suggesting that the operational debut of the first *Luftwaffe* turbojet-driven fighter, the Messerschmitt Me·262, could be imminent, the highest priority was assigned to the investigation of all possible interim countermeasures pending availability of a Soviet pure jet fighter*. A range of proposals for mixed-power fighters — aircraft in which the power provided by the principal engine of conventional type could be augmented by some form of less conventional auxiliary power unit — which had been considered over the previous two years immediately came under renewed scrutiny.

The application of ramjets and liquid-fuel rocket motors to existing fighters as a means of boosting performance was examined, but a more promising if somewhat longer-term scheme concerned a development known as the Khalshchevnikov "accelerator". Under development for some considerable time by the TsIAM (Central Institute of Aero Engine Construction), the "accelerator" comprised an engine-driven compressor which fed compressed air via a water radiator to a mixing chamber in which fuel was introduced under pressure by a battery of seven injectors, the mixture being ignited in a double-walled combustion chamber and then ejected through a variable orifice.

The Mikoyan-Gurevich OKB was, at this time, engaged in preliminary design of a jet fighter, the I-300, which was intended to be powered by two Lyulka-designed S-18 (VRD-3) turbojets. The S-18 had an eight-stage axial compressor, an annular combustion chamber and a single-stage turbine, but, in the event, official bench testing was not to be completed until the end of 1944 (at 2,866 lb/1 300 kg thrust) and the more immediate availability of the captured BMW 003 turbojet resulted in this being adopted in place of the S-18 for the I-300 which was to fly for the first time on 24 April 1946, eventually entering production as the MiG-9.

The I-250(N) mixed-power interceptor was one of the most innovative of Soviet experimental fighters. The photograph (left) of the first prototype shows the rather primitive clamshell-type shutters which sealed off the exhaust nozzle of the VRDK when not in use. The photographs at the head of this page and opposite depict the refined second prototype

Such was considered the potential of this "accelerator" as a means of achieving higher fighter performances that the principal fighter design bureaux were instructed, early in 1944, to initiate design studies for fighters embodying this development. From the proposals submitted, those tendered by the Mikoyan-Gurevich and Sukhoi OKBs were selected for prototype construction. In both the Mikoyan-Gurevich I-250(N) and the Sukhoi Su-5 — the prototypes evolved to meet the mixed-power fighter requirement — the VRDK (air turbo-compressor reaction engine), as the auxiliary unit was known, was mated with the Klimov M-107A 12-cylinder vee liquid-cooled engine and augmented the output of the piston engine by the equivalent of 900 hp for up to 10 minutes.

The I-250(N) was a small low-wing cantilever monoplane of all-metal construction. The wing was a two-spar structure and employed a low-lift TsAGI-1-A-10 section at the root translating to a -1-V-10 high-lift section at the tips, the trailing edge carrying Frieze-type ailerons and TsAGI slotted flaps. The dural monocoque fuselage accommodated the pilot well aft, in close proximity to the combustion chamber; engine air was taken in through an annular slot immediately aft of the propeller spinner and beneath this was a substantial intake for the compressor. Somewhat primitive clamshell-type shutters were used to seal off the exhaust nozzle in the tail when the VRDK was not in use. The lines of the fighter were, of necessity, somewhat corpulent owing to the considerable amount of space occupied by the VRDK ducting which dictated fuselage depth, and for the first time on one of its fighters, the Mikoyan-Gurevich OKB utilised a form of levered-suspension unit for the main undercarriage members. Armament comprised a 23-mm NS-23 hub-mounted cannon with 100 rounds and two 12,7-mm UB machine guns with 200 rpg mounted in the nose, one on each side of the compressor ducting.

The I-250(N) flew for the first time on 3 March 1945 with A.P.Dyeyev at the controls and at an early stage in the flight test programme clocked a maximum level speed of 513 mph (825 km/h) at 25,590 ft (5 800 m), this being only some 25 mph (40 km/h) lower than the maximum speed attainable at the same altitude by the Me 262 and it being calculated that the actual effect of the VRDK at that altitude was an increase in speed of 75 mph (120 km/h). Flight trials continued for some three months, terminating with the crash of the first prototype and the death of its pilot, Dyeyev, in June. A second prototype had meanwhile been completed, this embodying some minor aerodynamic refinements, such as an improved engine cowling lacking the long auxiliaries-cooling intake duct fairing featured by the first prototype, but by this time, the capabilities of fighters equipped with the VRDK were of little more than academic interest. Despite the promising results of the test programme, German forces had by now surrendered and, during the previous February, Yosif Stalin had ordered a 'crash' development programme for fighter airframes capable of utilising the newly-acquired BMW 003 and Jumo 004 turbojets. Thus, with

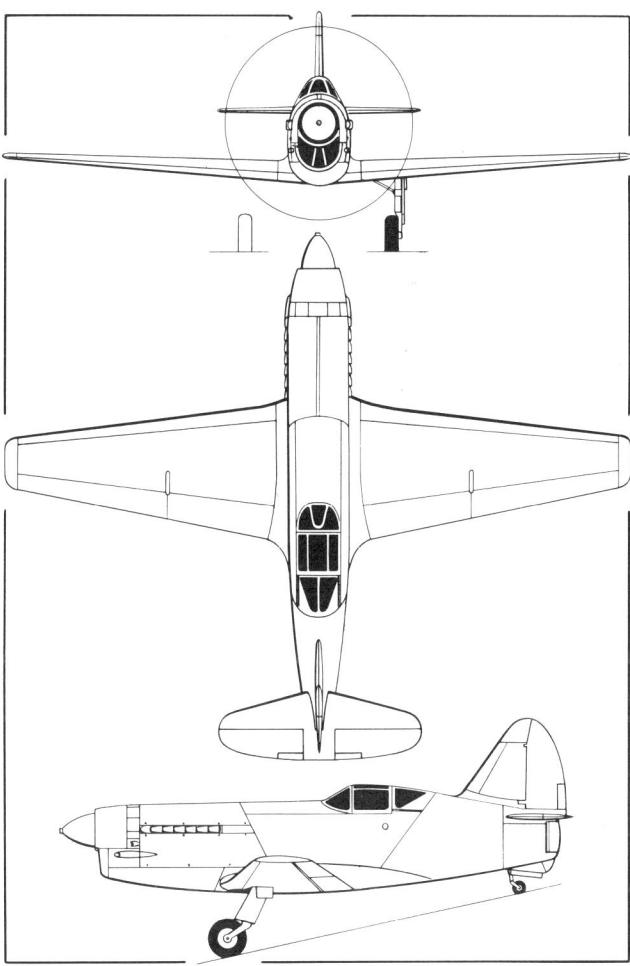

the destruction of the I-250(N) prototype, the mixed-power fighter programme was abandoned.

I-250(N) Specification
Power Plant: One Klimov M-107A (VK-107A) 12-cylinder vee liquid-cooled engine rated at 1,650 hp for take-off, 1,650 hp at 5,905 ft (1 800 m) and 1,430 hp at 14,928 ft (4 550 m), and driving a 10.17 ft (3,10 m) diam three-bladed constant-speed propeller, plus one Khalshchevnikov VRDK auxiliary unit affording 660 lb (300 kg) thrust for up to 10 min.
Performance: Max speed (combined power) 513 mph (825 km/h) at 25,590 ft (5 800 m), (VK-107A only), 438 mph (705 km/h); max range (VK-107A only), 1,130 mls (1 820 km); service ceiling, 39,040 ft (11 900 m).
Weights: Normal loaded, 8,112 lb (3 680 kg).
Dimensions: Span, 36 ft 3 in (11,05 m); length, 28 ft 8²/₅ in (8,75 m); wing area, 161.4 sq ft (15,00 m²).
Armament: One 23-mm Nudelmann-Suranov NS-23 cannon with 100 rounds and two 12,7-mm Berezin UB machine guns with 200 rpg.

NIKITIN-SHEVCHENKO IS-4

Perhaps the most bizarre of fighters under development during World War II was the so-called "folding fighter" — *istrebitel' skladnoi* — which was being tested in the Soviet Union at the time of the *Wehrmacht* onslaught. A variable-geometry or polymorphic aircraft of singularly radical concept, the "folding fighter" was conceived by one Vladimir V. Shevchenko, an engineering test pilot at the NII V-VS, and translated into a practical design by Vasili V. Nikitin, who was in charge of an experimental design bureau, OKB-30, which had previously been responsible for the design of a series of single-seat high-performance sporting monoplanes (NV-1, NV-2, etc) for the *Osoaviakhim* (Society of Friends for Assistance to the Aviation and Chemical Defence Industries) and a two-seat amphibious biplane (NV-4).

The "folding fighter" was conceived as a direct result of the controversy in the Soviet Union between the conventionalists favouring the tried and tested biplane formula for fighters and the visionaries who forsaw that the day of the biplane, despite its superior manoeuvrability, responsiveness and greater tractability, had passed and that the cantilever monoplane was the only possible configuration on which to base future fighter design. Vladimir Shevchenko, who had undergone engineering training at the MVTU Moscow Higher Technical School before joining the NII V-VS, believed that he had discovered a panacea — an aircraft that could be transformed from biplane to monoplane and vice-versa at the volition of its pilot.

The fighter combining the short-field and low-speed characteristics of a lightly-loaded biplane with the high-speed performance of a more heavily loaded monoplane was indeed radical in concept, but Shevchenko was convinced that an innovatory warplane such as he envisaged was within the capabilities of state-of-the-art aircraft engineering and this view was shared by Vasili Nikitin with whom he discussed the project and who promptly initiated a design study for a "folding fighter" along the lines proposed by Shevchenko. This project was submitted to the GUAP (Chief Directorate of the Aviation Industry) in November 1938, and thus was set in train one of the most extraordinary experimental fighter development programmes ever launched.

Despite the general consensus that fighters designed along more conventional lines would be most likely to produce worthwhile results, the project received the qualified approval of the GUAP and detail design began early in 1939 as the IS-1 — *istrebitel' skladnoi-1*, a full-scale mock-up being mounted in one of the TsAGI wind tunnels to ascertain the effects of retracting and extending the lower wing in flight and to calculate the amount of hydraulic power necessary to retract and extend the wing rapidly. The tunnel programme, completed in the late autumn of 1939, suggested that translation from biplane to monoplane and back to biplane in flight should not present the pilot with any insurmountable handling problems assuming symmetrical movement of the two halves of the lower wing. Any assymmetry during wing movement, on the other hand, would, it was predicted, result in forces beyond the pilot's ability to control. Nikitin was fully confident that the prototype, construction of which had proceeded in parallel with the tunnel investigation, incorporated ample safeguards against assymmetry and in April 1940 the IS-1 was completed.

The IS-1, which had earlier been assigned the

The IS-1 (left) was, in its time, one of the most extraordinary single-seat fighters ever conceived, being an early example of variable geometry. Of singularly radical concept, this polymorph could translate from biplane with fixed undercarriage to cantilever monoplane with fully-retracted main undercarriage members at the will of its pilot. The first translation from biplane to monoplane and back in flight was effected with this aircraft in June 1940

(Right) The general arrangement drawing illustrates the IS-1 "folding fighter" in both biplane and monoplane configurations, the undercarriage remaining extended when the fighter was flown as a biplane

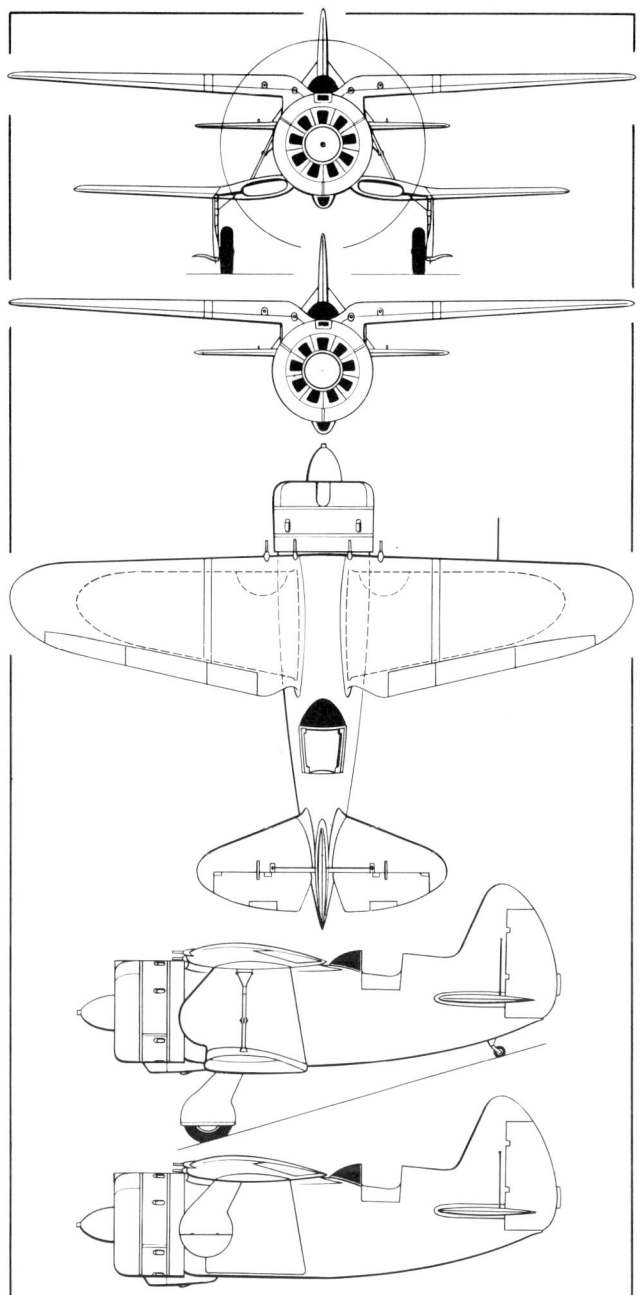

designation I-220 under the official system then in use, was essentially a test bed intended to prove the basic concept and little effort had been expended on aerodynamic refinement. A cantilever sesquiplane for take-off and landing, the IS-1 was of mixed construction with a welded steel-tube fuselage covered by dural panels forward and birch *schpon* aft, the upper wing being a two-spar metal structure with dural skinning and the retractable lower wing being a plywood-covered wooden structure. The movable control surfaces were metal framed and fabric covered; power was provided by a Shvetsov M-63 nine-cylinder air-cooled radial rated at 1,100 hp for take-off and 900 hp at 14,765 ft (4 500 m), this driving a three-blade variable-pitch propeller; provision was made in the gulled centre section of the upper wing for an armament of four 7,62-mm ShKAS machine guns with 1,000 rpg, and overall dimensions included an upper wing span of 28 ft 2 in (8,60 m), a lower wing span of 22 ft 0½ in (6,72 m), an overall length of 22 ft 3 in (6,7 m) and an undercarriage track of 8 ft 11⅞ in (2,74 m). With the lower wing extended for take-off or landing, total wing area was 224.21 sq ft (20,83 m²), and with the lower wing retracted wing area was reduced by 37.6 per cent to 139.93 sq ft (13,00 m²). At normal take-off weight of 5,071 lb (2 300 kg), wing loading was thus increased from 22.62 lb/sq ft (110,44 kg/m²) to 36.24 lb/sq ft (176,94 kg/m²).

Each lower wing half was hinged both at the root and at the mainwheel leg attachment point, and to translate from biplane to monoplane configuration after take-off, the down latches holding the inboard section of the lower wing rigid were released and the section was drawn upwards and inwards by means of a simple system of ram and radius rods actuated by means of a hydraulic jack on the fuselage centreline, oil pressure being supplied by an engine-driven pump. While the inboard wing section described an arc of approximately 90 deg to lie flush in recesses in the sides of the fuselage centre section, the main undercarriage member was simultaneously raised vertically to occupy a well in the underside of the retracted inboard lower wing section and the outboard wing section was drawn into a recess in the upper wing. This process, which occupied 7-10 seconds, was reversed to restore the aircraft to biplane configuration, and the system was so designed that asymmetric retraction or extension was impossible. The interlinking of lower wing and undercarriage movement meant, of course, that the latter could not be retracted while the aircraft retained biplane configuration.

The first in-flight translation from biplane to monoplane and back to biplane was undertaken in June 1940 by another NII V-VS engineering test pilot, Georgi Shiyanov, who shared the initial test programme with Vladimir Shevchenko, and several leading Soviet test pilots were subsequently to fly the IS-1, including Stepan Suprun and Aleksei Grinchik. The hydraulic retraction and extension system functioned efficiently — an emergency hand pump was provided but was not to be needed during the test programme — and no untoward handling problems were encountered during translation. Being intended solely to demonstrate the feasibility of the "folding fighter" concept, Nikitin had made no attempt to design the IS-1 for high performance, the maximum speed in monoplane configuration being only 281 mph (453 km/h) at 16,075 ft (4 900 m), an altitude of 16,405 ft (5 000 m) being attained in 8.5 minutes. However, Nikitin had already "productionised" the IS-1 design by the beginning of 1941 as the IS-2 (alias I-220bis), this embodying some aerodynamic refinement, and had

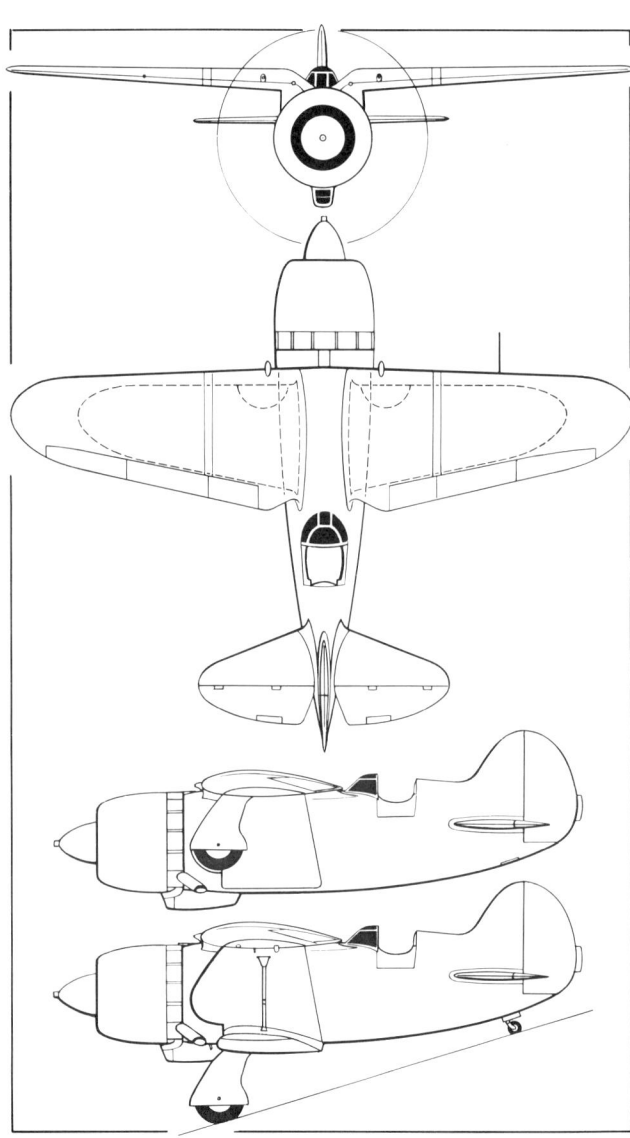

(Above and left) The IS-2, a refined development of the IS-1. The bottom side profile depicts the aircraft with lower wing and undercarriage extended

taken the "folding fighter" programme an ambitious stage further with the very much more advanced IS-4.

The IS-2 was a straightforward development of the initial aircraft, featuring some structural refinement, redesigned vertical tail surfaces and a close-cowled 14-cylinder two-row Tumansky M-88 radial of 1,100 hp for take-off. The inboard ShKAS machine guns were retained but the outboard weapons were replaced by 12,7-mm Berezinas. Nikitin was aware that the potential performance of the IS-2 would not compare favourably with more conventional fighters by then under test but he believed that the IS-4 would compare more than favourably. Like the IS-2, the wings of the IS-4 were essentially the same as those of the IS-1, but from this point the similarity ended. Aiming at the highest possible performance, he had elected to design the IS-4 around the experimental M-120 16-cylinder liquid-cooled engine, which, apparently of X-type, promised a maximum continuous rating of 1,650 hp. This was to drive a 10.17-ft (3,10-m) diameter 3SMV-1 three-bladed constant-speed propeller. The cockpit was to be enclosed by an aft-sliding canopy and the armament was to comprise a similar combination of ShKAS and Berezina synchronised machine guns to that mounted by the IS-2. The radical retractable wing arrangement was coupled with what was, for the Soviet Union at that time, the almost equally radical feature of a retractable nosewheel undercarriage which was still viewed as a dubious American innovation.

Construction of the prototype IS-4 was in its final stage by the beginning of 1941, but in the meantime, the development of the M-120 engine had been abandoned. It had been calculated that, with the M-120, the IS-4 would attain maximum speeds of 271 mph (436 km/h) as a biplane and 447 mph (720 km/h) as a monoplane, service ceiling being estimated at 41,000 ft (12 500 m)

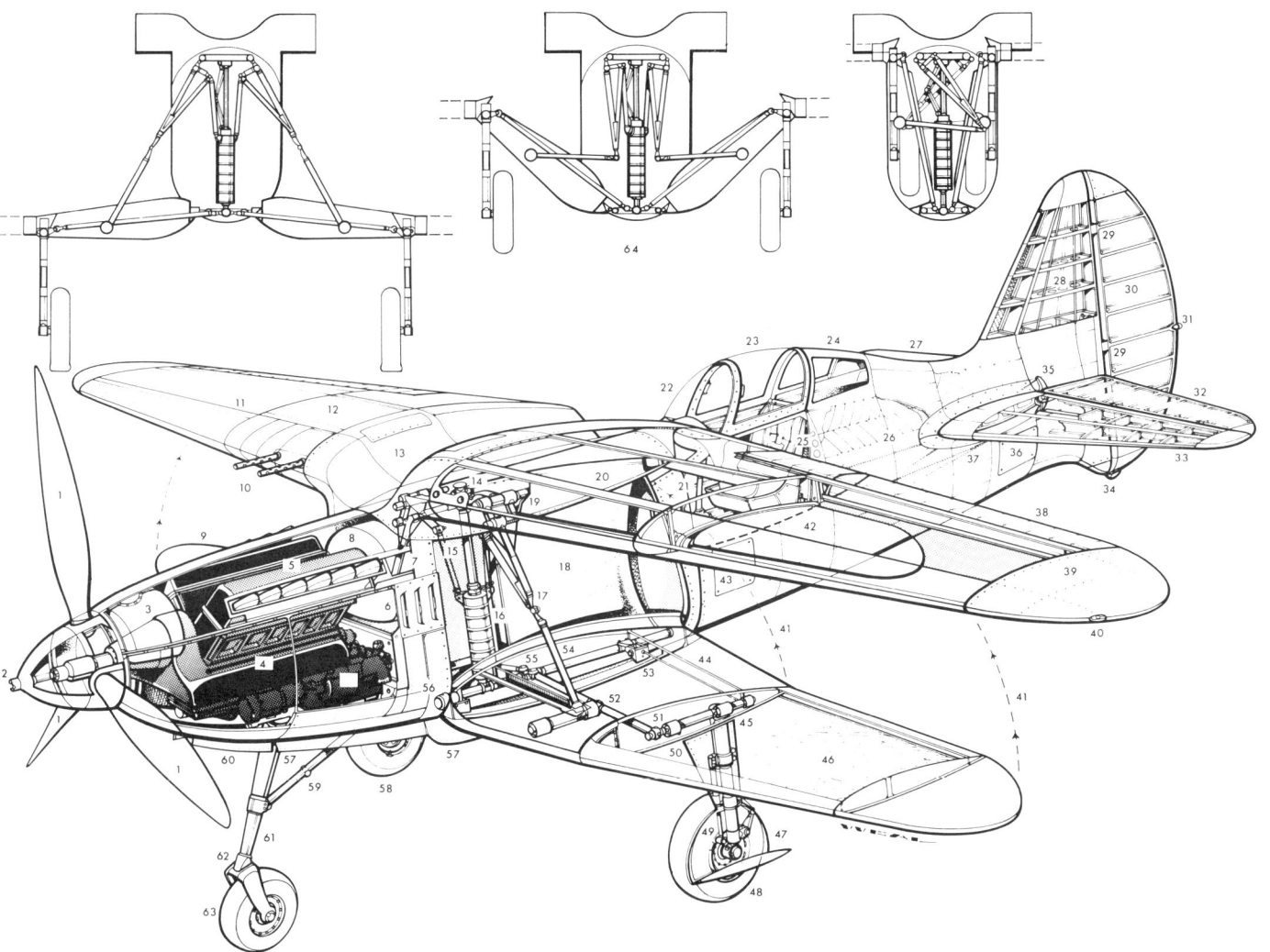

Nikitin-Shevchenko IS-4 schematic drawing
1. Three-bladed variable-pitch propeller
2. Starter dog
3. Header tank
4. Mikulin AM-37 12-cylinder liquid-cooled engine
5. Exhaust stubs
6. Cooling louvres
7. Starboard lower wing retraction strut
8. Oil tank
9. Starboard lower wing
10. Armament (7,62-mm ShKAS/12,7-mm Berezina)
11. Two-spar metal upper wing
12. Dural skinning
13. Gulled wing centre section
14. Hydraulic jack/retraction strut attachment
15. Starboard retraction linkage (forward mounted)
16. Port retraction linkage (aft mounted)
17. Retraction strut hinge point
18. Fuselage centre section recess
19. Retraction pivot mounting
20. Wing profile
21. Control column
22. Curved one-piece windscreen
23. Cockpit canopy
24. Aft fixed glazing
25. Pilot's seat
26. Shpon aft-fuselage skinning
27. Starboard tailplane
28. Tailfin structure
29. Rudder hinges
30. Metal rudder frame (fabric covered)
31. Rear navigation light
32. Metal elevator frame (fabric covered)
33. Port tailplane structure
34. Tail bumper
35. Elevator control
36. Access panel
37. Control cables
38. Wing flaps
39. Dural skinning
40. Port navigation light
41. Retraction arc
42. Underwing recess
43. Access panel
44. Undercarriage cable
45. Mainwheel leg pivot
46. Plywood lower wing skinning
47. Mainwheel hinged fairing
48. Port mainwheel
49. Brake assembly
50. Undercarriage leg fairing
51. Undercarriage linkage/lock
52. Undercarriage retraction link
53. Lower wing inner section rear hinge/downlatch
54. Retraction strut lower section
55. Wing centreline pivot
56. Lower wing inner section forward hinge/downlatch
57. Nosewheel door
58. Starboard mainwheel
59. Nosewheel retraction strut
60. Nosewheel leg door
61. Nosewheel leg
62. Axle fork
63. Aft retracting nosewheel
64. Simplified schematic of wing retraction sequence (front view). Note starboard strut hinges across face of hydraulic jack, port strut across rear

and landing speed at 66 mph (107 km/h). The IS-4 retained the same 28 ft 2 in (8,60 m) upper wing of the IS-1 and IS-2, but the span of the lower wing was increased to 23 ft 3½ in (7,10 m) although the gross area remained constant at 84.28 sq ft (7,83 m²). Thus, at a calculated loaded weight of 6,393 lb (2 900 kg), the IS-4 would have had a wing loading of 28.51 lb/sq ft (139,20 kg/m²) in biplane configuration and 45.69 lb/sq ft (223,08 kg/m²) as a monoplane.

No liquid-cooled engine of comparable power to the M-120 readily presented itself, the most suitable alternative being the somewhat heavier Mikulin AM-37 12-cylinder vee rated at 1,400 hp for take-off, and the IS-4 prototype was duly modified to accept this power plant. That this highly radical fighter *was* flown in the summer of 1941 is known, but records of what flight testing was conducted were apparently lost when the rapid advance of the *Wehrmacht* necessitated the hurried evacuation of Nikitin's experimental design office and adjacent workshops, the "folding fighter"

(Left) An artist's impression of the proposed M-120-engined IS-4 variable-geometry fighter showing the wing and undercarriage in the final stage of retraction. The general arrangement drawing also depicts the IS-4 as originally projected for the M-120 engine, the lower profile illustrating the aircraft with AM-37

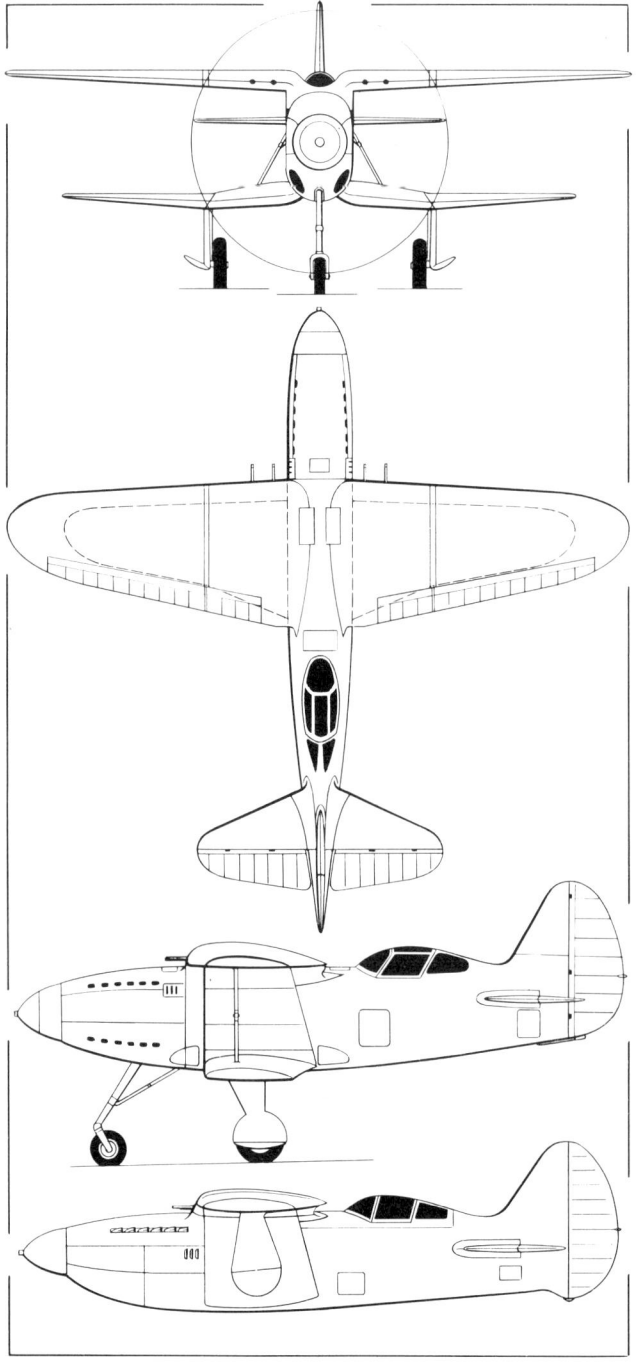

prototypes being disassembled and crated for transportation and their ultimate fate being unknown.

The exigencies of the times now dictated concentration of all effort on production of the maximum number of orthodox "frontal fighters" in the minimum possible time and the investigation of the unorthodox was temporarily dispensed with. Thus, in the latter half of 1941, the "folding fighter" was adjudged too long a term programme to warrant its continued pursuit. Furthermore, doubts had been expressed concerning the satisfactory maintenance of such a radical warplane under frontline field conditions. It was believed that a nosewheel undercarriage would be unsuited to conditions appertaining at most V-VS operational airfields — a belief that was soon to be disproved by the successful operation of the Bell P-39 Airacobra from these fields by the V-VS; it was suggested that the retraction and extension system employed by the lower wing would be prone to battle damage with the loss of the fighter as a result, the pilot being unable to land the aircraft in monoplane configuration, and while it was admitted that the handling characteristics were perfectly acceptable when the aircraft was being flown by an experienced test pilot, it was suggested that rather higher skill than possessed by the average V-VS pilot, with his somewhat cursory formal training, was likely to be called for.

Vladimir Shevchenko had by this time been reassigned to operational duties with the V-VS as a major commanding a night fighter regiment, but Vasili Nikitin was loath to totally abandon what he considered to be a highly promising concept, continuing the design development of "folding fighters" alongside work on more orthodox projects, producing more than a dozen further design studies for progressively more advanced "folding fighters". In the event, none of these was to progress further than the drawing board or wind tunnel model testing, for, despite the ingenuity that they undoubtedly displayed, they were simply too exotic to obtain adequate support for their continued development at a time when the principal advantages that they offered over more orthodox fighter monoplanes were no longer considered of such paramount importance as when the idea of the "folding fighter" had been conceived. Thus, during the course of 1942, further work on what were undoubtedly the world's first variable-geometry fighters to have flown was finally discontinued.